NOTES FROM THE MIDDLE WORLD

NOTES FROM
THE MIDDLE WORLD

BREYTEN BREYTENBACH

Haymarket Books
Chicago, Illinois

First published by Haymarket Books in 2009
© 2009 Breyten Breytenbach

Haymarket Books
P.O. Box 180165
Chicago, IL 60618
773-583-7884
info@haymarketbooks.org
www.haymarketbooks.org

ISBN: 978-1-931859-91-2

Trade distribution:
In the U.S. through Consortium Book Sales and Distribution, www.cbsd.com
In the UK, Turnaround Publisher Services, http://www.turnaround-uk.com
In Canada, Publishers Group Canada, www.pgcbooks.ca
All other countries, Ingram Publisher Services International, ips_intlsales@ingramcontent.com

Cover design by Ragina Johnson
Cover image from "A Long Walk to Freedom," by Breyten Breytenbach, 2009

Special discounts are available for bulk purchases by organizations and institutions. Please contact Haymarket Books for more information at 773-583-7884 or info@haymarketbooks.org.

This book was published with the generous support of the Wallace Global Fund.

Library of Congress CIP Data is available.

Entered into digital printing May 2018.

CONTENTS

To the memory of Mahmoud Darwish

Lucidity is the wound closest to the sun.

—René Char

This morning, for the first time in a long time,
the joy again of imagining a knife twisted in my heart.

—Franz Kafka

All our secret is in survival.

—Jacques Derrida

DANCING

it is going to be tough
to forsake this earth
(but who or what goes away?)
the terrible spaces of dispossession
always yours alone

dark hill over there
like a bowl of shimmering light
with trees still bearing the signs of wind
in joint and wound and miracle of breath,
and here a mudslide
slopes and plains
and black vegetation

all suffering is distance –
how could you know of people in the mud?
what is lived? what seen, heard
or merely imagined,
and what matters?

when walls crumble
and the unimpeded cry
opens in you
a pealing, shimmering incantation
of dancing spaces –
a wind silence

One

MAKING BEING

On Arts and Culture

First man moves, then he reflects, and then he encircles with words the things seen.

It has always been peculiar to European cultures—not unique, but preponderantly so—to conquer, subdue, explore, expand, and exploit; later to maintain the conquered territories as sources of raw materials or as potential markets; to loot and gut the cultures found there, and then to collect their "artifacts" so as to "understand" the broken toys, the images and the relics of a broken spirit, and ascribe a "meaning" to them. Anthropology, ethnology, even our modern-day "multiculturalism"—however noble and generous the attitudes of the people involved—are manifestations of greed, the urge for power over the rest of the world, the need to catalogue the "Other" and relegate him to a position of being at best, "untouched by time," but always inferior. It would seem that the West has to undo in order to comprehend.

A softer side to this pornographic policy of conquest and appropriation of the "Other" motivated by Western needs now clothed in the exigencies of a global market economy would be the contemporaneous effort to promote "exchanges," to "protect him against the rapacious West," to provide him with the means to autonomy and "authenticity." This is by and large the Western affliction that has shaped and profoundly malformed the world; its latest expression is the Bush doctrine that reaffirms the arrogance and the purported *right* of the powerful to subject the world to the spreading of freedom—"for its own good," we are told sanctimoniously, but in fact for the base appetites of global power.

As an African, I find it demeaning that the outside world should come to catalogue, study, and "understand" Africa and its art; I find it equally objectionable that Africa's artistic expressions and attempts to shape a history and an identity, now more by way of denouncing our endemic corruption and the failure of our governing and economic systems, should then be patronized as exotic examples of freedom and magic. These approaches are never innocent and they are not unbiased; it cannot be done without the baggage of cultural assumptions bred from specific histories and conditions brought by the protagonists. The crudeness of the conditioned measuring tool assessing our differences ultimately destroys the object of investigation; the unexamined paternalism of the do-gooder finally humiliates the adopted artist.

I bring no answers to the questions of how cultural relations between the North and the South ought to be conducted or even whether they need to be formulated at all. However, I believe movement forward lies in the way we put the questions. Truth lies in the road (maybe in ambush), for how can we prejudge the contours of the destination that will be shaped by our getting there? Traveling creates its own landscapes, and that goes for the migration of ideas as well. The reassuring thing is that one does always end up with a destination. Naturally, on the way out, as maverick mortal, I'd be inclined to say "we *must*," "we *ought* to"; I'd even be inclined to stitch my own speculative "truths" as patchwork lining inside the dark and suffocating coat of Certainty, if only to use as secret maps.

Instead of providing answers and purveying "truths" my intention will be to say something about the problematic of art and culture in Africa at *present*, and how these express or interact with notions of identity; therefore about the connections between artistic creativity and identity consciousness and the tension between arts and politics.

I am taken back to an experience I had a number of years ago, it must have been October 2003, when I visited a major show of African masks, artifacts, and other ritual objects in Rio de Janeiro. The exhibition was organized by the Goethe Institute and financed by the Banco do Brasil, and consisted of pieces culled from German anthropological museums. I was upset and angry to find those magnificent shards and fragments and remnants of largely interrupted traditions—saved from termites and mold, it is true, although still imperceptibly stained by the mystery of time—now alienated from the kingdoms where they were made and cleansed from their native surroundings, removed from the sacred groves and therefore turned away from their intended functions. "Statues, like men, were made to die," Alberto da Costa e Silva wrote in an excellent text illuminating the exhibition.

I remember that part of what lit my gut to sputter was a "justification" reproduced in the catalogue. It quoted a text found in the Archives of the Ethnological Museum in Berlin:

> At times such as ours, which with a rough hand destroys countless primitive tribes and furrows the surface of the earth in all directions ... (we are) responsible to coming generations to preserve as much as possible of that which still remains from the ages of humanity's childhood and youth [in order] to aid the understanding of the development of the human spirit. What is destroyed now will be irredeemably lost to the future.

One should not even bother to italicize words (concepts?) such as "primitive," "responsible," "coming generations," "humanity's childhood," etc. But what shameless paternalism! Who gave the cultural predators of the North the right to custody of the cultures of others?

In that same "justification" one may read in passing how fifty thousand objects looted during the war by the Soviets from German museums were returned from St. Petersburg following the reunification of Germany, and one knows sadly that no "artifact" or "fetish" would ever be considered as having been stolen from Africa and therefore a return is out of the question. (Yes, but if these were handed back—to whom and under what conditions? How does one give Africa back to itself when it depends on handouts for survival? The indignity and injustice of depriving these objects of a "native" or "home" death will remain until such time as Africa can reassert itself and reclaim its heritage).

◆

Why were these works, torn from their environments of "collective altars or domestic shrines"—*dixit* da Costa—kept in ethnographic museums and not simply exposed as the works of art they are among other artworks of the world? Can it be that they'd be out of place in an art museum because we've forgotten that all art is related to the sacred?

Thinking back now on that exhibition, I'm reminded that the problems and equations around identity and responsibility and magic and sharing probably always existed. For, apart from the quite stunning formal and inventive beauty of the pieces I saw there, I was struck by their power. Nearly every object had a singular *presence*. Even when abstract, strange, or with gaze averted, their there-ness continued to speak and to interrogate us. They spoke of power and of sacrifice, of the unsayable also—but more importantly, in this attempt to bridge the gap between life and beyond-life (or other life, or other-than-life) they told us about the fears and the dreams, sometimes futile, of being alive. In fact, they were mute or stilled manifestations of identity. Maybe this is the magic of the human condition: to be poised on that cusp of a cry of anguish and shout of defiance; to know that we are finite and fragile, and yet strive to communicate with the silent stillness of otherness. And in this there is communality beyond the demarcations of the ages, of styles, of other allegiances and interpretations.

Movement precedes thinking is a tenet of Tibetan wisdom. It is, in my limited experience, a physical imperative to *move* if you want to think. We have to be in motion for the thinking to take shape and not the other way around. Static thinking (plotting, cogitating) before implementing the ideas normally denotes another process—rather, a different hierarchy of intentions. When thinking precedes movement it is usually informed by control, by the intended search for given solutions—and this can lead to the establishment of dogma. Down this road may beckon the manipulation of perceived identity within larger contexts for purposes of power politics. The obverse may be that when movement initiates and opens thinking we are not only courting the possible advent of the unknown (*that*, after all, may be upsetting and inhibiting)—but we are also putting ourselves in a humble or learning relationship to the knowledge and experiences of others. We bring, we test, we transmit, but we also change and allow ourselves to be changed.

In the movement of thinking (and sometimes of thoughts) and in the thinking awareness of physical and/or cultural displacement, or at least of its potential, artistic creativity is born. Artistic creativity is the movement of perceptions, of bringing about new combinations of past and present, of realizing how *new* the *old* can be (and sometimes how prematurely old and static the purportedly new is), of projecting future shapes—and thus helping to shape the future. This is done through interactions with other cultural expressions or the expressions of other cultures, by reciprocal imitation, by undergoing influences. Those who are often feared and even detested by society, because, as da Costa put it in the catalogue, "they control fire, wood or words," undertake these travels, sometimes to the end of the night.

The questions I'm trying to bring into focus do not have fixed outlines; rather, their positioning and possible elucidation are subject to accelerations provoked by events and new or modified insights—Africa is always changing—or sometimes they gather in eddying pools of reflection, maybe stagnation: another reason for *moving*, if only to shatter the surface image and to rid oneself of the stench of self-serving bullshit in the nostrils. Chekhov wrote in his *Notebooks* that the dead do not know shame, but that they stink terribly. To be alive is to keep moving, even as a carrier of shame.

And when one says *movement* one is talking rhythms and patterns, contrasts and contradictions and contestations, maybe conflict, hybridism and survival consciousness, the intensified interaction between the known and the unknown. Uncertainty is written on the horizon of the nomad. The sky with its lines of invisible stitching to nothingness becomes a familiar companion—always respected, sometimes feared. Breaks and jumps will jolt you awake, as brief loss and questioning and enlightenment. You will be like an old Amhara at morning prayers when it is still dark over the hills, resting your chin in the fork of your long staff, dozing off because of the acrid smoke and interminable prayers, to crash from meditation to the fucked-up-ness of the world.

Identity is then a vector of interaction.

"Who are you?" will be the first question. You turn around, look at yourself, and wonder, because the question is unfair. Is he speaking to *me*? Isn't identity the ultimate intimate stranger?

The rest is culture. I mean: it is the residue and the backdrop of the known. Culture is the receptacle of the riches of received (or stolen) certainties. Certainty, as we know, easily slides into Orthodoxy (with a nudge or two from those with vested interests), and this Security is customarily hoisted on a pedestal as Truth. Truth, strangely enough, even when enshrining the expression of shared convictions (*"Truth we can believe in,"* as CNN might say), must be only and One to survive. It can brook no bastards. Diversity is not Truth's favorite lover. It has weak loins and feels threatened by that which has a propensity for abandoning itself in lovemaking the better to encompass and suffocate you. It is very difficult for Truth's power to imagine being divided or shared. Hence the potential—indeed, the predisposition—for conflict and the glorification of the manly virtues of combativeness and possession.

One could perhaps argue that "culture" is the other shape of identity, another plane of the mask, larger and shared (we all have it): reassuring us because it makes us all alike as if hewed from one trunk. All thinking has been thought then, and movement will now be merely exercising the figures of conquest and of submission, if need be five times a day facing the East.

How do we in Africa go about fostering appropriate linkages between creativeness on the one hand and the challenges of managing the tensions associated with citizenship and identities on the other? How can we strengthen the civic role of the arts in relation to the politics of citizenship and identity? How, and in which ways, can narrative (private and public histories) be recognized as constitutive of identity?

What are the complex relationships between man and the spaces of his past and his present?

Is the enactment of the holistic nature of human existence and its relations to the Other constituted by creative activity? We are the only animals, as far as we know, who imagine and invent ourselves. We seem to need this projected dimension, this *dépassement de soi*, in order to survive; also, to remember ourselves and thus to commemorate the ancestors and to talk to them. We could say that this link to the "sacred," if that is what it is, by itself creates a sense of shared identity. Art may be our way of darkening the communal threshold by trying to cross it, making of it something more problematical than just a wedge of wood in the shape of a deaf coffin. The unattainable elsewhere may be at the root of our sense of incompleteness and therefore of much existential suffering, and we need art to make that sense tangible and, thus, bearable.

Or do we entertain this striving in order to imagine ourselves different, to have an afterlife waiting so as to finally escape from the innate cruelty that has us killing one another for neither cause nor satisfaction? Is art—the expression of communal and individual imagination—but a whistling as we pass through the plundered and littered cemeteries of the killing fields?

Not only Africa, but in some ways the whole world, is in turmoil. Powerful forces are redesigning the frontiers of morality or simply erasing them in the name of "security," "faith," and "civilization." We are all of us creaking and cracking under the pressure of globalized greed and a homicidal lust for power draped in the pious pretensions and the moth-eaten purple cloak of "One-God" religion or "democracy." Democracy is killing us; at the very least we are choking as it is stuffed down our ungrateful throats.

A gorged goose will eventually gag on the good garbage presented as the substance of the right to happiness.

Is this manipulation by the greedy? Or are we to assume that the cataclysms I talk about, like templates pressing against one another, are but blind forces of history fortuitously accompanied by cliché-spouting generals and "dry drunk" presidents who, like flies on the coach, brag and smirk about the dust they're raising in the Iraqi desert?

Africa is part of the world—as subject, not as actor. Africa is defined by its weaknesses. The bane of Africa's public life is the twisted relationship between power and appearance: the less real power of thought or of influence we have, the more important the appearances and appurtenances of privilege become through posturing and protocol. With the need to prance (really a camouflaged expression of impotence) come hyperbole, grandstanding, demagoguery, the manipulation of myth and prejudice, graft and corruption and nepotism. Our presidents try to rinse the blood from their tunics and promote themselves from warlords to living effigies of the idols as if they could thereby incarnate the masks of the ancestors. And they do so in the name of cultural exceptionality. (If only we could exile and confine them to the glass encasements of that show I saw in Rio de Janeiro!)

The *excuses* for the parlous state are ready-made and cynical: historical processes, injustice and inequality in the world, and especially racism. (Note: I'm not saying these factors do not exist; I'm just refusing to accept them as faits accomplis, as intractable matter that cannot be molded and overcome.)

And naturally, as we see every day, the corruptors abroad are only too keen to continue exploiting the situation. The rich nations of the world spend a gross nine hundred billion dollars a year on fabricating and selling defense equipment: a lot of the so-called "small" arms will turn up in Africa's equatorial forests and deserts to be used for killing the hungry.

Thereafter the rich nations will collect contributions to reform the child soldiers and teach them how to sing together, to lift the mines, and to provide artificial limbs.

We are part of the world. Yet, in Africa, we are both watching world events from the sidelines and engrossed in our own conflicts and ways of falling behind. We seem to be caught in a contradictory movement of searching for larger unity with greater impact and efficiency and the enhanced potential of bringing about sustainable self-sufficiency (perhaps mistakenly embodied as an investment in more comprehensive, flaccid units like the African Union), while experiencing the breaking up of known certainties—our societies ostensibly "freed" by the ideologies of "independence" and of "liberation." Running like a theme through this contradictory movement is the unbridled greed of the powerful and their wives and offspring, and the total acceptance, it would seem by everybody else as well, of the lemming imperative of materialist consumerism.

Surely, we cannot possibly accept that our sense of ourselves as a continent should be that of being sidelined, mired in underdevelopment, caught in the madness of wars and armed uprisings as the only way out—exploited, humiliated, and getting poorer! And, as surely, our way to experience ourselves cannot be defined by imitating the materialism of the West!

"Identity" and "citizenship"—both of these are spaces. (By "space" I mean that area or interstice in time—and of course, sometimes it is geographical—where something is allowed to exist or come about.) In the case of citizenship the space is the state and/or the nation. These are not the same and they do not necessarily overlap. The Kurds constitute a nation without a state. The Gypsies are a people without borders of their own. The Palestinians are allowed territories—they want to think of these as a "state" but they consist of a series of ghettos that are now, more and more, concentration camps where they can be cornered like rats, despoiled, and killed with greater ease.

(The outside world will be indifferent. Out of sight, out of mind as long as it doesn't affect the stock market.)

Are the Fulani a nation? And if so, how does their nationhood intersect with existing states? Can we say that one finds with Rwanda two nations within one state? What is one to make of Thabo Mbeki's assertion that in South Africa you have two nations—one poor and black and the other rich and white—when there are now numerically more rich black people than white ones? (He would however be right to point out that, percentage wise, there are still far more rich whites than blacks and infinitely more poor black people; in fact, more so than under the previous regime. If he wanted to be honest he could also note that the gap between rich—"new" and "old"—and the old and newly poor is growing. He may further note and wish to comment on the interesting fact that on an average the Indians who had been brought there by the British as indentured labor now constitute the richest population group in the country.)

A state ought to be a vessel for the rational exercise of legitimate power and the arbitration by a public administration of the interests of large composite communities living within "natural" borders demarcating a certain cultural cohesiveness. But the states we have in Africa were largely colonial constructs and fancies, handed over to loyal though alienated local elites who were to assure good governance and the continuation of profitable "native" exploitation.

The nation is another kettle of *capitaine*. To me, the very notion of nationalism is an artificially bloated and toxic extrapolation of identity awareness. It is nearly always used to whip up sentiments against the others within and without, the non-nationals, those with the burned countenances or the pale visages. (I'm tempted to say, in the American framework, the "Guantanomese.") It is the sick outgrowth of the existential need to imagine the self as group animal, now given potency because offered a larger hate-space within which to fudge its better instincts and transform its anguish and uncertainty into animosity.

It is remarkable how wishful thinking can create the opposite of what it wants to achieve: When José Marti claimed that there were no "bad" or "good" Cubans but only the badness of not being Cuban, or that there were neither "white" nor "black" Cubans but only Cubans, he helped bring about a situation that would lead to exile, and to where the occulted prevalence of racism to this day on the island cannot be discussed. And when we in South Africa declared national reconciliation and *simunye* ("one nation"), that it was all over but for the blaring of the trumpets and the crowing of the entitlement cocks, the national debate was effectively stifled with results that may still come to haunt us.

But there is also the growing space of civil society in Africa. Who can pretend that there's any single state in Africa that can honorably cover its commitments to its citizens—in terms of basic expectations like sanitation, education, transport, security, communication? National security there will be, yes *baas*, mostly exercised against perceived fractious counterforces among the citizenry, and our soldiers will be trained in the art of repression by American "advisors," to fight the people, as all opposition to presidential power must be "terrorist." So who then takes up the slack in providing services and development? Multinationals and transnationals do not administer states (despite the presence of Elf, Shell, and Exxon): they run presidents and pay armies. The nearest thing we have to foreign regency practically directing state options and functions would be the IMF and the World Bank—the "Bretton Woods

Institutions" as we so prudishly call them (as a palimpsest of the "Berlin carve-up"). The cash flow allowing for citizens to survive will in practice transit via gougers and gangsters. In Guinea-Bissau, the minister of finance is effectively the business lady disbursing "expatriate remittances" at exorbitant service fees through the local Western Union.

In reality, many segments of civil society already serve as relays for national or state administrations. Is this a good development? To what and to whom ought the NGOs be held accountable? To the donors? Or do they have to give account to those segments of the population whom they serve? (In Senegal, for instance, we have an autocratic steal-all president who would rather not have any NGOs at all operating in the country, particularly as he starts cooking the next national elections. Is he not there to receive all money and disburse some to those whom he wishes to bribe?)

◆

And then there are the spaces of creativity—of the artists, the intellectuals, the women, the revolutionaries, the Africanists. What movement do they generate? What ethics do they incarnate? What are their values? Can we claim that creativity in Africa is a vector for modernity cutting across the scarred borders, and that this is simply a necessity for survival and development and *not* some underhand aping of imported "Western" ideas—survival, in other words, in the face of the retrograde influence and vaunted "authenticity" of those "nation-states," churches, and other conservative *confrèries*, which are but vehicles for the peddling of power and patronage and corruption?

In Africa, the many movements of varieties and realms of creativity (growing from language and idealism and the ritual magic of music and visual imagination, in other words, from the need to transform the given "reality") both undermine or negate the cohesiveness of "state" through internal questioning and supersede its borders by identifying with the larger aspirations of unity.

Does it mean we can do without states and live outside nations? Of course not. We need them—as reasonable and legitimate demarcations of administration and responsibility, as agencies of stabilization, as forms and forces collectively mandated to allow for and to guide development. After all, can we possibly wish for Africa to fall apart even more, to develop further black holes? Even the West doesn't like black holes, however far away and indigenous they may be: it complicates controlling the extraction of diamonds and other strategic minerals.

We should be acutely aware of the existence of different spaces in Africa, and that by their very being they induce movement. For, ideally, a space is not a refuge or a sanctuary, but a place of metamorphosis. And as keenly we should recognize the progressive dialectical movement that will come from the development of spaces of creativity, however critical they may be, and their interaction with the common good of shared national values. This much-needed acceptance of diversity is not only good for progress; it is also the guarantor of a shared identity.

The above concepts were behind the "Poetry Caravan" organized by the Gorée Institute a number of years ago. Ten African poets from various parts of the continent—Tunisia, Mali, Ivory Coast, Zimbabwe, Senegal, etc.—traveled together from Dakar to Timbuktu by car and train and pirogue. Each night a local festival involving griots and musicians and poets from the region was held where we stopped. Poets from one place would join the caravan for as far as the next camp and along the way there would be "workshops" in translation and local languages and customs. It was a conscious attempt to reactivate old trade routes and the art of passing words from one marketplace to the next, like dreams and visions on the wind. A film was made of the trip called *Tara, The Paths of the Word*.

"By yourself you travel faster, but you go further in the company of friends," a Touareg sage, as old as varnish, murmured in the night. "And if you move from place to place in this fashion, influencing and being shaped, you are no longer a foreigner in the place of arrival," his companion responded.

◆

By now, Reader, you will have noticed that my relationship to the notion of "culture" is rather like that of an angry dog to its image in the mirror: I bark and I piss against it. It is because I think of it as a vessel-word, a vassal to meaning, and a mere growth intended to achieve an objective. That's why I'd rather qualify it as an additive to, say, a *culture* of nationhood, a *culture* of peace, a *culture* of creativity—that is to say, the conscious *cultivation* of these. It ought to be a practice and a process, not just a product of the *culture* of Culture, which is public, political, and often putrid.

To this could be added a *culture* of interaction between South and North. The movements between North and South—with different motives—cannot be stopped; it is ancient, it has always involved a transfer and a transmission of experiences and sometimes of expertise. But the time has come to rethink its modalities, purposes, and effects, and to identify new ways of experiencing the exchanges.

Culture is still the result of creativity, however stultified by respectability the expressions we now pay homage to may be, or however much they may have been made trite and maudlin by the noncritical glorification of whatever passes for exotic or different. It ought still to be about enacting freedom, also by those artists and artisans who are carrying on a tradition that serves its own purposes and its own community, and thereby extend the best humanist traditions. Freedom should not be a privilege; it is an unquestioned continuation of being, but also a duty, as well as the enactment of moral hygiene.

The best way to assist transformation through cultural means in Africa would be to help empower the individual to test all limits through the invention and investing of creative spaces. We need to rethink Africa. Such thinking (the *movement*, the *space*) will be a creative process of imagination. It will revitalize memory as the instrument for revalorizing old or "local" solutions to the problems of arbitrary power abuses and the stultification of prejudices.

It will be movement: Africa has always been movement. ("The masks were made to be seen in movement," da Costa writes.) It will foreground and enhance the reality of the inherent multiplicity and pluralism of identity—private and communal—as release for active and creative tolerance and acceptance, and thus for growth. It will be a space of excellence—no special pleading, no wallowing in being victims, no "blame me on history" syndrome. It will promote modernity (I'm talking of common sense, decent values and systems and structures—secular, if you like, but "popular" and motivated and rooted, and sacred in its tranquil aspirations). It will recognize the enrichment of hybridism.

We need to consciously bring about the spaces where artists can provoke a necessary "dialogue with the other"—the opponent, the oppressor even—for one must be in the position to *donner langue*, to "give word" if one does not want to die of the highly infectious dead tongue and white eye disease.

For, the same way as everybody else, we in Africa need to learn and relearn how to *see* the world, how to *live* in the world, how to *behave* in the world. Maybe we should remember that our art forges tools for change and constitutes objects encapsulating change, that it indicates ways of becoming other and making other; and as well that our art is perhaps a way of losing possession of useless certainties. It may lead to the paradoxical satisfaction of being able to say with the old Touareg whom I met in the night: "I do not own myself, I've given myself away." (He might as well have added that, "what you cannot give will be lost.")

And so, as African citizens, we have to claim a number of rights and admit to our responsibilities (just as you should in the North): the right and the duty to be critical, the right to participate in public life, the shared responsibility for spaces of common good, the responsibility for and the right to imagination, the responsibility also to recognize how nefarious intellectual and even artistic activity or "freedom" may become when we lose our bearing on the ethical star. (Who else but depraved intellectuals and their political buddies developed the horrific notions of "ethnic cleansing," "exterminating the cockroaches," "ivoir-ité," and "Apartheid"—to name but a few "glorious" fruits of the mind?)

Our dignity will be reestablished by the modesty, but also the tenacity and the ethical intentions of our *processes* of creativity and the viability and relevance of our *products*.

My night visitor reminded me that an Arab philosopher of the Twelfth century, Ibn al-Arabi (a Spanish convert and wanderer if I'm not mistaken), already knew: "The origin of existence is movement." And that movement is a prerequisite for finding sound shared morals.

Two

MANDELA'S SMILE

Glimpses from the Mirror of our Time

I did not struggle to be poor.
                    —Smuts Ngonyama, Spokesman, African National Congress

We need to develop the ability to embrace uncertainty from a position of intelligence and imagination. The more of us who admit to our vulnerabilities, the more trusting the public space.
                    —Njabulo Ndebele in a recent interview in *City Press*

The state of emergency in which we live is not the exception but the rule.
                    —Walter Benjamin

Dear Madiba,

This is the year of your ninetieth birthday; the whole earth is celebrating—to excess I am tempted to say. Why? Because we cling to you, Nelson Mandela, as a living icon, as a liberation hero who did not renege on his commitments to freedom from oppression and justice for all, as the father of the rainbow nation, as a man of nearly incomprehensible moral resilience who walked out of prison after twenty-seven years of harsh incarceration and forced labor seemingly without bitterness or a thirst for revenge, and who is still giving unstintingly of himself. And I would add: because you are a wise and curious and caring humanist with so much humor and such a lovely smile …

I, too, want to celebrate your achievements, your example, the frail dignity of your old age. And yet when a South African newspaper approached me to be among those invited to address you publicly on this occasion, I balked. Why? Partly, because I find it obscene the way everybody and his or her partner—the ex-presidents and other vacuous and egomaniacal politicians, the starlets and coke-addled fashion models, the intellectually challenged and morally strained musicians, the hollow international jet set—treat you like some exotic teddy bear to slobber over. You have become both a *vade mecum* and a touchstone: those who touch you—but it must be in public and caught on camera— believe (make believe) that they have now been edified to a given moral rectitude. Of course they pay for it—exorbitant sums, I'm told. (Not for nothing your nickname, "Moneydeala"!) After all, your aura is for sale, and your entourage is very needy and greedy. I expect your many years of apprenticeship must mean that you see people for what they are, be they friend or foe, and that you are immune to sycophancy. Still, did you really distinguish between comradeship and obsequiousness? Your sense of fidelity is legendary. And I don't think your self-deprecating humbleness is faked. Why, then, tolerate the scroungers, the charlatans, and the chancers feeding off you?

Why did you opt to bilk the rich—who are only too keen to pay and be seen to *share*, for charitable purposes or out of "base" instincts to protect their larger business interests, and thus cheaply identify with and benefit from a suggested correct political stance in the new dispensation? Was blackmail the better way of extracting the riches and privileges to be distributed? Were they vulnerable because they felt some *guilt* about the ways in which they accumulated their wealth? And was the possible alternative—socialist redistribution—too horrible to contemplate? Too horrible for whom? Or did you do this because you believed there was no other possibility of finding urgently needed support for the very poor and destitute, or to advance the positions of those close to you? Or was this perhaps also just an expression of the prevalent materialist values of the world, and you didn't want to strangle the geese producing golden eggs?

Forgive me if I do not discern the forest of deeper initiatives for social change because of the grandfatherly tree of easy gratification everybody wants to be seen stroking or carving his initials into. Sometimes I think our problem is not so much that we're supposed to have come to "the end of history," but that historians no longer have the voice or the incentive to decrypt and transcribe an understanding of the events and movements shaping our world.

In due time there will probably be an assessment of your political career and the impact you had as president of the country—and you were nothing if not a consummate politician. Your being the historical vector for controlled compromise and change may ultimately be equated with statesmanship. Already we know you saved us from civil war.

This should be remembered as your single most important legacy, and we must never forget how lucky we were. Some will say you could only do so by aborting the revolution.

But my own unease, now, is of a slightly different kind. I wish to express my deep affection for you. You are in so many ways like my late father—stubborn to the point of obstinacy, proud, upright, authoritarian, straight, but with deep resources of love and intense loyalty and probably with a sense of the absurd comedy of life. A cad also, when tactical considerations made it necessary. I think I've told you this.

And now you are very old and fading. ("The word of the voyage is subject to the wind." —Edmond Jabès.) It is not our custom to remonstrate with an honorable man going into that night that awaits us all. Even less so in Africa, where it is assumed that extreme old age brings wisdom and should be venerated. And yet—all along I respected you as a man of integrity and of courage; all along I felt I could disagree and say so, even when my insights were uninformed and my positions unwittingly partisan. Why would it be any different now? Am I to assume you have gone soft in the head? Should one, for the sake of worldwide euphoria, because we *need* to believe in human greatness, avoid sharing one's confusion and disappointments with you?

Again, my respect and affection for you can only be expressed in telling what I see and understand of this country. You could be my father; you were always a mentor and a reference; you are also a *comrade*.

◆

I am talking of where we are now, in 2008.

Recently, I had the occasion to spend some time in South Africa. I don't get to go there very often anymore, and I realize the extent to which I'm no longer able to "read" the environment instinctively. I've lost touch, maybe because the surface is so often slick with blood. I also realize that, like so many others, I've become conditioned by expectations of the worst. The seemingly never-ending parade of corrupt clowns in power at all levels, their incompetence and indifference, indeed their arrogance as historic victors drunkenly driven by a culture of entitlement, the sense of impending horror in the air because of the violence and the cruelty with which crimes are committed, to be tortured and killed for a cell phone or a few coins—one becomes paranoid. I was getting more scared the longer we

were in the country. I was beginning to calculate the statistical chances of
being the next to be robbed, raped, or blown away.

The circle narrows. The grandmother of a close friend—she's as old
as you are—pleads with her robbers not to be sexually violated, she even
claims to be infected with a communicable disease; the nephew of a fellow writer is shot in the face, killed in his own house by a night intruder
whom he mistook for a rat; the son of my eldest brother is stabbed on a
parking lot outside a restaurant, the blade pierces a lung, the police never
turn up, he is saved because his companion calls her boyfriend all the
way in Australia by cell phone and he could summon a nurse he happens
to know in Johannesburg. (The woman is on a first visit to the country;
she leaves the next day and swears never to return.)

Behind the everyday bloody shadow play there are tendencies that
I'd like to talk to you about, for although it would perhaps be unconscionable to ascribe any part of responsibility to you for the ambient
lawlessness, there are deeper problems related to power and to the
value of human life that must have been evident all along. But, as ever
when one visits the country, what sears the mind and chokes the heart
first are the apparently random events that have become emblematic of
a society in profound disarray.

◆

I come across a report on school violence, from Johannesburg, pro-
duced by the South African Human Rights Commission (SAHRC).
Games such as "hit me, hit me" and "rape me, rape me," in which
schoolchildren chase each other and then pretend to hit or rape each
other are being played at South African schools, it says. The commission heard from Community Action Toward a Safe Environment

(CASE) that "this game demonstrates the extent and level to which brutalization of the youth has reached, and how endemic sexual violence has become in South Africa."

The report says school is the "single most common" site of crimes such as assault of students and the second most common for robbery of pupils. According to a study conducted by the Centre for Justice and Crime Prevention (CJCP), young people were twice as likely to become victims of crime than adults. "Just over two fifths (41.4%) of the young people interviewed had been victims of some form of crime."

The CJCP found that toilets were an area of the school feared most by pupils.

More than a fifth of sexual assaults of young people occurred while they were at school, and according to a study conducted by the Thohoyandou Victim Empowerment Programme (TVEP) among 1,227 female students who were victims of sexual violence, 8.6 percent were assaulted by teachers. The Western Cape Education Department established that "very often, disciplinary procedures are not followed through and educators resign upon being formally charged."

Another study, found that "26 percent of students were of the opinion that forced sexual intercourse did not necessarily constitute rape."

The Red Cross Children's Hospital in Cape Town told the commission the most common forms of violence it treated students for were assault with a fist, knife, or panga, rape, and sexual assault, bite wounds, and firearm-related injuries.

I'm talking at such length about this because one of your foundations intends to help save the children, Madiba—and your love for the little ones is heralded. Indeed, doesn't your benevolent smile, known by billboard all over the world, tell us to be compassionate to the children? How do we turn the culture of child abuse around?

Johannesburg, again:

The mother of a two-year-old boy, who was found in Kagiso on Friday with his genitals mutilated, has been located ...

"Police managed to find the boy's mother, Meisi Majola, 26, who reported her son missing from 14:00 yesterday [Thursday]," said Inspector Solomon Sibiya.

"She said her son had disappeared from their home in Roodeport on the West Rand."

The little boy, dressed in a maroon track suit, a gray track suit top, and *takkies* [sport shoes], was walking around in tears in the Ebumnandini informal settlement in Kagiso, when he was picked up by two men.

They stopped their car and noticed that his takkies and pants were stained with blood. Sibiya said the child was taken to a police station where it was later discovered that he had been mutilated.

To be used for *muti* would have been the purpose, as you know: human ingredients for a potion against the despair of living.

"Police could not find out where he lived as he was too traumatized to speak. Now that his mother has been found, we would be able to conduct a proper investigation," Sibiya said.

Do you know what constitutes the nightmare fear of young, middle-class men in South Africa these days? To be arrested for speeding or being under the influence and thrown into a cell with hardened criminals—as often as not now infected with HIV/AIDS—before being released a few days later.

A young man goes out to celebrate one last time with his male friends before his wedding. On the way home he is caught for reckless driving. The police cells are dark. All night long he will be sodomized repeatedly. His screams of anguish and pain elicit no reaction from the police. The next morning, at first light, one of the perpetrators sidles up to him, strokes his forearm, and whispers, "After last night, you are truly one of us."

Have we tried hard enough to give another meaning to "brother-hood"?

How did we get to the point where the dead are mutilated, the right eye gouged out in morgues to be used in concoctions that will make the sight of the living more acute and where corpses are unearthed so as to steal the coffins?

The saddest case may be that of the four young "Colored" farm children ages nine to thirteen, barefoot, thin like praying mantises, clutching one another as they appear in court for having stoned to death one of their playmates, a girl of eleven, ostensibly in a fight over a bottle of cheap sweet wine. Or, as another report had it, because they thought she had AIDS. When she no longer moved, they ran to fetch an adult. In court they would rub one dry and scabbed foot over the other, whisper, look around with big eyes. ("Give me your eyes. And the separate will be one." —Edmond Jabès)

◆

During the recent stay, I was invited to participate in the annual literary festival Time of the Writer, organized by the Centre for Creative Arts of the University of KwaZulu-Natal in Durban. It was good to be back in the Elizabeth Sneddon Theatre, which I remembered from the first events years ago, and it was a pleasure to congratulate Peter Rorvik, the director of the Centre, and his colleagues for what they had achieved so powerfully. In that bright and tumultuous early period of liberation, two friends from the long-ago past of struggle and exile came to personify Durban for me—Mazisi Kunene, the prophetic poet of Zulu epics now somewhere among the spirits, his teeth bared sardonically, and Lewis Nkosi, the sharp and fearless novelist, present on this night where I had to make the opening remarks. Both had tried to capture the complex realities of South Africa in words; both attempted to find the strong words that could hold new dreams of justice. Together we had emptied countless bottles in repeated brave but futile efforts to assuage the anguish.

I believe that a venue where readings and discussions take place regularly will become imbued with the patina, the sacred spirit, of creativeness. People come over the years to propose and to explore writing, and debate the underlying assumptions. What brings them together is a shared passion for exploring the ways these concepts may affect the social environment in which we live. And what you have as a result is this space of many voices where, if you close your eyes, you may still hear the rustle of arguments and the shaping of imagination to clarify commitment.

◆

Nietzsche wrote: "And moreover, what, after all, are these conventions of language? Are they possibly products of knowledge, of the love of truth; do the designations and the things coincide? Is language the adequate expression of all realities? ... Only by means of forgetfulness can man ever arrive at imagining that he possesses "truth" ... [One] designates only the relations of things to men, and for their expression he calls to his help the most daring metaphors ... Every idea originates through equating the unequal ... What therefore is truth? A mobile army of metaphors, metonymies, anthropomorphisms—in short, a sum of human relations, which became poetically and rhetorically intensified, metamorphosed, adorned, and after long use seem to a nation fixed, canonic, and binding—truths are illusions of which one has forgotten that they *are* illusions."

◆

Of course, the illusionary "truths" I proposed that night were not original; they were informed by insights of the ancestors and the experiences of contemporaries such as you, and maybe I twisted them to fit my anger and my pain. My own contribution, I said, when looking ˎ at what is happening around us, may be pessimistic, brutal, arbitrary, and generalizing. It was important at the outset, therefore, to put on record that there is also reason to celebrate. Only too often do I forget that the struggle for dignity is a complex and never-ending process. Even now, there are still diligent hands writing and beautiful voices speaking out for compassion and honesty and clarity. These too ought to amplified and encouraged.

◆

Madiba, you will be remembered for being naturally curious and compassionate about the lives of the people you came in contact with and for the way you put everybody at ease. I know you would have listened to my story, however personal. Don't even the most generic and sweeping statements have their origin in private events?

We, my wife and I, had been in the country for little over a month then, and it was an unsettling experience. We'd spent much of the preceding few weeks clearing out the house in the Little Karoo where we used to live for shorter and longer periods over the years. It was heartbreaking, in that leaving is the confirmation of a failed experience and a broken dream—the "dream" was probably my own naive expectation that a new dispensation ushered in by a liberation movement would realize at least some of the objectives we fought for: economic justice, an ethical public life … And for me it was the end to the possibility of *belonging*—writing and painting in a studio overlooking a riverbed where wind scythed and swayed the reeds, where yellow and red birds flitted, where giant mountain tortoises would come to scrape their shells against the white wall around the house, and from the mountain slope on the opposite bank baboons and shy-hoofed buck and rock rabbits would come down in the gray light of dawn. Ah, for the naturalness of growing as old as you under that sun, bone-white like a bleached thorn in summer, glinting like snow on the inland mountain peaks in winter! In the cemetery there were swellings of earth covering the bones of people with familiar names.

Clearing house was disturbing because I had to sort through files and manuscripts and throw so much away. And I came across, in notes and letters and snippets of essays, the recurring references to barbaric criminality, the plague of raping, theft, and fraud, the indecent enrichment of the few, manipulation, redeployment as a form of impunity, public office as an exercise in scavenging, the breakdown of essential services, entrenched and continuing racism, the lack of public morals or even common sense.

Why did I not see the picture more clearly? Had I become inured to the social and economic realities of the country? Could I not read the pattern? Was my understanding obscured by the dream, the desire for freedom?

I must tell you this terrible thing, my old and revered leader: if a young South African were to ask me whether he or she should stay or leave, my bitter advice would be to go. For the foreseeable now, if you want to live your life to the fullest and with some satisfaction and usefullness, and if you can stand the loss, if you can amputate yourself—then go …

◆

Should we not be engaged in trying to see the world at large and Africa in particular as clearly as possible? We know that "seeing" is also an act of imagination and, particularly, that in the present void with its absence of horizons of expectation, we need to explore and promote a collective moral space and the fearlessness of creative thinking shot through with the doubt brought by uncertainty in order to be of use to the younger generations. By imagination do we become part of the surroundings.

This may sound contradictory, but I tried to formulate an approach to this idea during an earlier meeting of Africans involved in artistic and cultural facilitation at the Gorée Institute off the coast of Dakar. Some of the people in the theater on the opening night in Durban had taken part in that workshop; to them my ruminations must have sounded like a refrain.

In the workshop, we from the institute proposed an open-ended endeavor:

Imagine Africa. And then: to start making it concrete through specific actions, even if small. To "Imagine Africa," we suggested, is simply, among other meanings, the recognition of the dialectical relationship between the imaginary and the real. I take it as common cause that part of the human condition, maybe the essential flame, is the process of imagining ourselves. *We are who and what we are only in becoming.* We survive; we live because we conceive of the nature and the purpose of being. Our consciousness is invention, or recognition bounded by the possible.

This is not unique to the human species. After all, do birds not imagine their territory and perhaps also the nature of their being through flight and song? Animals come to an experience of themselves through movement leaving traces as markers of memory. A lake must imagine its surface. It could be that life is awareness because it knowingly strives for imagining existence and thus must question the sense and the finality of the process. Leaving traces of ourselves, as in creative productivity, or in what we saw when the wind swept through the reeds, could then be read as part of that definition of consciousness. To progress we must strive for something just out of reach, for the parabola as a tail of light left by the Southern Cross—if only for an existence that will be more compassionate and decent than the cruelty, paranoia, greed, narrow corporatism, or narcissism we mostly indulge in and find such ample justification for.

And so we dream. There's the personal dream to come to terms with the inevitability of being finite (and perhaps never understanding your smile); there's the communal one of justice and freedom upon which we hope to secure the survival of the group. And then there is the dimension of a moral imagination.

But what if grotesque black-and-white pictures of death flood the imagination?

◆

This is our world. We *know* no more than people before us did. You who come from what seems an unbroken line of ancestors linked by praise songs—do you agree? What will be the last song you hear? The chanting of warriors as they breast the final hill? Every generation lives in the fullness of its own comprehension, the completeness of its own smiles. And our minds are as ever bordered by darkness, except that we now live in an infinitely more dangerous place. But by the same token, I think you have taught us, we cannot indulge ourselves—for reasons of political correctness or tribal guilt or cynicism or common greed—in the rainbow intoxication of knowing and understanding *less* than those before us did.

What is *our* horizon? Globally, that behind the burning fields as smokescreen of worldwide insecurity we encounter poverty—endemic and brutalizing and deepening—and the greed of the insatiable predators: the arms manufacturers and the oil guzzlers and the smugglers of people. That, at the core of our barbaric new age, however much dolled up by the gadgets of modernism, we find fundamentalists exterminating thousands of innocent people as "collateral damage" from despair for what they believe to be the cause of their cruel and jealous god. That, in demagogic chambers of states claiming to be liberated and democratic, the cynical rule unrestrained in their lust for power and profit. That, in the whitewashed institutions of our so-called enlightened societies, we see the same obdurate and institutionalized discrimination against women. And, Madiba—yes—that at the heart of this deep forest of cruelty we still lack compassion for the children.

What we experience in Africa may not be worse than other parts of the world. Maybe our problems are just more acute and intractable. A new American president may well close down the penal colony of Guantánamo and start recognizing and making up for the war crimes committed in Iraq and in Afghanistan, even if only to secure U.S. access to oil; the rulers of China may one day be obliged to start looking after the interests of their peasants and workers and to stop polluting and cheapening the world; even Israel may conceivably be prevailed upon to desist from exterminating Palestine as an entity and start giving back what they have stolen.

Maybe *our* problems have deeper and more obdurate causes. Who in Africa is going to put an end to the impunity of the criminals ruling over us? Who is going to resolve the genocide in Darfur and the mass raping of women in the Congo? Who in Africa is going to face the consequences of something like 120,000 child soldiers? How are we going to come to terms with the fact that our nation-states are a fiction for the benefit for our dictators and their ruling clans? Who is going to get back the money our politicians stole from the people? Who is going to take responsibility for condoning the rule and extending the protection of international legitimacy to a maniac like Robert Mugabe? And how are we going to stop this seemingly irrevocable "progress" of South Africa to a totalitarian party-state?

Should the International Criminal Court hold Omar Hassan al-Bashir accountable for attempted genocide in Darfur? Yes! Should Robert Mugabe and his blood-besmirched, murdering acolytes be indicted for crimes against their own population? Yes! Should Bush and Cheney and Rumsfeld and Rice and Wolfowitz likewise be brought before a world court and charged with international war crimes? Of course! Bush must be entitled to as fair a trial as Saddam Hussein had. (The only difference between the two of them is that the effete American has the personal courage and honor of a barroom peacock.)

More importantly now for us, old master: Did you, did we, ever seriously intend to bring about a democratic dispensation in South Africa, with its checks and balances and accountability? Or was it about settling old colonial scores? For how long can we continue on the schizophrenic knife edge between the discourse of equality and justice and the practice of plundering and arbitrary power? For how much longer can this double-talk be sustained, to the population and to the outside world? How come the individual human life has no value? Is this traditional? Do you know that "national liberation" is destroying, by debasement and abuse (as it did in Algeria, Angola,

Guinea-Bissau ...), our dream for an African modernity nourished from African roots and realities? Why do we call "national democratic revolution" the process by which the state and all its institutions—and, by extension, culture and the economy—become the feeding trough for the Party and its cadres? Was it ever conceivable that a national liberation government could cede power if outvoted? For how much longer are we going to be playing the role of "victims of history?" For how much longer are we going to demean ourselves by living on handouts from the rest of the world? How do we deal with the humiliation and the shame? For how much longer are we going to allow for all our policies and decisions to be dictated by the paralyzing pain of centuries?

You know all of this, even though you will talk of a million points of light to obliterate the darkness I'm speaking of. How dare I even suggest you are not aware of what and how we are? Will you not point to the example of *one life*, lived with full consciousness and responsibility and honor, as an irrefutable answer? Yes, but how can *people* change the profound cultural apathy?

◆

"This is our world. Fiction/Imagination is an unveiling of what we didn't know we knew." I was quoting this, that night in Durban, from a literary accomplice in another life and world, because I wanted to draw the furrow between the open source (some would say a sewer) of our imagination and the land of reality we try to work. In so doing, I said, we write into and from the preexistent underground of images, memories, thoughts, etc.—"uncovering" what that companion called *"the shared Atlantis of the imagination."*

I will never know what goes on in your mind, or what that shield of a smile behind which we try to advance should tell us. I have no idea how the experiences you went through changed your intimate landscapes. Maybe you only thought of yourself as the instrument of a particular historical moment? What do you hear when all is quiet—the dancing feet of your warrior tribesmen on the green hills of Qunu so disfigured by soil erosion? The acclamation of the world?

Perhaps we know no more than those who preceded us, but it is as true that we have to transcend our limitations, that we must cling to the notion of a utopia (call it "clean and accountable government" or "common sense") as justification and motivation to keep on moving and making a noise. For the mind has to dance, even with death, if we want to stay it from reverting to despair and narcissistic self-love. To survive, we must assume the responsibility of imagining the world *differently*.

Imagination gives access to "meaning," I argued that night in the theater. Storytelling is a system of knowledge; a swarm of words on the page aggregates "authority"; the very act of narration carries a presumption of truth. And I'm only too aware of the fact that I position myself to you as a *writer* trying to imagine you, or at least the meaning of your smile. Is imagination not the first expression of identification and therefore of generosity? Writing as the production of textured consciousness is the mediating metaphor between fact and fiction. It is in the movement of the heart-mind and the thinking awareness of physical and/or cultural displacement that creativity is born—as sequences of perception bringing about new combinations of past and present, projecting future shapes and thus helping to shape the future. We are hardwired to see *intention* in the world, and thus predisposed to the art of learning by intervention. We become by making. We realize ourselves through acts of transformation. And these journeys bring with them implications of accountability. By imitating the forms of creativity we apprehend the contents of *meaning*; in the enactment of ethics we learn about the prescriptions and limitations of the will to have being emerge: together these constitute the freedom way.

It's a long walk to freedom. (And, to quote Edmond Jabès again: *"Distance is light, as long as you keep in mind that there are no limits. We are distance."*)

I tried to empty myself before the mirror. I know I'm getting to resemble my father more every day. When I look at you I'm reminded of the unbridgeable distance between my father and me, but also, how I can now begin to experience him from within. And in that way I'm getting closer to you. Age may bring closure, an unclothed closeness, but also a blind raging against darkness. You will almost certainly not read this "letter"; others will hold me accountable for having dared to draw you into my writing.

But I'd like to think (imagine!) you'd agree when I say we must go on, we need to leave the reassuring and self-caressing domain of the "possible" to extend the reach of the impossible/unthinkable (such as, respect for the sacredness of the individual human life in a country like South Africa, whatever the pains of the past and even despite the brutalization of injustice and of poverty). And these ethics, this neutrality, demand that one allows emptiness for a certain moral imagination to come about—that is, spaces for the promotion of doubt and for the unexpected, even and perhaps especially for what we as writers did not expect to find but always with compassion for the weakness and the human dignity of the other.

In the interview Njabulo Ndebele gave to *City Press*, with which I started my letter to you, he also says:

The South African of the future will live comfortably with uncertainty because uncertainty promises opportunity, but you have to be robust about it, you have to be thoughtful about it, you have to contemplate it to get the full richness of it, and I think that is the challenge of being South African: to run away from unidimensional and definitive characterisations of ourselves ... The capacity of the country to imagine the future depends on nurturing imaginative thinking from the beginning of a child's life right up to the end. We've somehow given all that up along the way ... We need to develop the ability to embrace uncertainty from a position of intelligence and imagination. The more of us who admit to our vulnerabilities, the more trusting the public space.

When some years ago a few writers visited Mahmoud Darwish, the Palestinian poet who died this past August, in the besieged ghetto of the West Bank, he spoke to us of the role of poetry. He ended by saying:

It is true that all poetry stripped of another life in another time is threatened by a quick dissolution in the present. True that poetry carries its own future and is always being reborn ... But it is as true that no poet can put off for later, in some other place, the *here* and the *now*. In our time of storms it is a matter of the existence, the vital energy of poetry ... To give life to words, to give them back the water of life, can only be by way of bringing back the sense of living. And all search for sense is a search for the essence which confounds itself with our questioning of the intimate and the universal, that interrogation which makes poetry possible and indispensable, that questioning which has as consequence that the search for sense is also a search for freedom.

◆

Dear Madiba, I'm aware of how unfair it is to lay all of the above at your feet, like some birthday bouquet of thorns. You deserve to have your knees warmed by a young virgin as old King David in the Bible did—not pummelled by the likes of me. Already that opening night in the Elizabeth Sneddon Theatre in Durban, I tried to assume my pessimistic approach by saying that I'd come neither to praise Caesar nor to bury him but to ask what he has done with the trust of the people! By "Caesar" I meant the African National Congress or "liberation," not you. Can the two be separated? Is it ever thinkable that you would denounce the ANC? Would you consider the thought that your organization has lost the way—or did we try to look away from its innate Stalinism and greed because of the heady struggle for release? It is a harsh question; it may even suggest that we have only the ashes of spent dreams to poke around in.

But of course I believe that with accountable leadership and the full and recognized participation of what used to be known as the "live forces" among the population, this continent can be turned around, and with it South Africa. Our dreams *can* be realized—and when I say this I very much have in mind the examples of Steve Biko and Robert Sobukwe.

I dream, as I want to believe you have dreamed, and I will continue to strive, for an integrated continent of generosity, economic justice, creativity, civil and civic responsibility. A continent that will develop its own sustainable modernity far away from Western "universalist" models of globalization serving only the masters. A continent that knows its primary riches is its diversity of cultures. A continent whose citizens will stop blackmailing and whitemailing one another and the world with politically correct subservience and the "blame us on history" syndrome. A continent that will understand the sense and the importance of the public good. A continent that will stop begging and stealing, and where the totalitarian conflation of nation and state and party in power will be abolished, where dictators will stop killing their people for their money and where prancing will be confined to the catwalks of fashion shows. A continent where the ancestors are alive, certainly, to dance with—the way you used to dance on the stage, even in your old age, hoping to catch the fancy of the ladies! A continent that will never again accept second-class citizenship and will be neither the playground for Western phobia or self-interested charity nor the dumping ground of Chinese junk. A continent that will respect and celebrate life—the life of the planet. A continent that will plant crops and feed itself. A continent that will eradicate small arms and have no purpose for acquiring submarines and where the criminal and corrupting sleaze brought about by fabricating or buying arms will be stopped. A continent that will be the guardian of the past, all the pasts, and the custodian of our future—and where we will *know* that the future lies with the women. A continent of profound *métissage* and thus of reciprocal enrichment. A continent where no racism will be tolerated—and by that I also mean the racism and the humiliation of poverty.

Perhaps I will then, too, accede to a wider wisdom—of the kind that I sometimes heard or surmised in your words. I remember seeing a distant echo of what may be possible reproduced on a large photo of a scene in Africa, in the bar of the Hôtel Nord-Pinus in Arles, where I went recently to meet up with Mahmoud Darwish again. Outside the streets were blindingly white with sheets of heat, nearly as if under an African sun, but inside the bar it was cool and dark. The writing on the photo, giving it the veracity of nervous movement, was by the hand of Karen Blixen and came from her book *Out of Africa*. She talked of the natural fearlessness and grace of her guides, "this assurance, this art of swimming, they had, I thought, because they had preserved a knowledge that was lost to us by our first parents; Africa, amongst the continents will teach it to you: that God and the Devil are one."

◆

I know there's no need to justify my *lèse-majesté*. However much you may disagree with my analyses, you would have heard me out. Besides, I believe we writers, word-makers rooted in civil society, need not be the clowns and the fools of those in power—not even the "whites" among us who suffer from being excluded from the "black" world. In fact, I believe we should think freedom of the mind as a conscious and constant attempt to *unthink* order and authority. To think *against* hegemony of any variety, including the liberationist and the nativist and the iconic—particularly the insidious, moralistic mawkishness of political correctness expressed as a sightless idolization of our "leaders." To think *against* the dictates, the values and the property of consumerist societies. To think *against* the laziness of narcissism.

We need to remember that we are bastards and forget that we're supposed to be obedient citizens. Indeed, that our absolute loyalty lies in the disobedience to power and in our identification with the poor.

◆

With abiding respect, and because I believe that smile was also sometimes a mocking one,

Your mongrel son,

Mshana

Three

OBAMANDELA

The Prophet of Black Folk said:
History is a marriage
between the image
and the meaning

—Adonis

First it was the voice. It seemed to proceed from a similar hollow in the chest as that of the old man. A voice with *coffre*. Sounding somewhat sepulchral. Certainly somber. A blue voice. Resonant.

I was listening to Barack Obama and the tonality, the pitch, the cadences particularly, were reminiscent of the voice of Nelson Mandela. There was a likeness in the diction too—a hint of cumbersomeness of the tongue. As if they speak neither easily nor just for the pleasure of making sounds. More remarkably, they both express themselves in full sentences even when off the cuff. Sentences you can transcribe and print as is without having to snip the *um*s and the *aw*s. As they begin to speak, they both seem to know where each following sentence, covering a thought, is going to end. (A saying in Rwanda explains, "If you take your time, you can cook an elephant in the pot.")

41

Mandela's voice tends to be higher, and his accent sometimes has an echo. This may be due to bad sound systems in the open air of South Africa.

They speak with emphasis, as if they know the weight of their own minds. They are, after all, *serious* people. The words are seldom original in reference, inventive in imagery, or, for that matter, provocative in thought—this is no Charlie Parker blowing his horn. What is conveyed, however, is a solemnity of purpose and a kind of self-evident morality that needs to be expressed. ("The word that remains in the mouth becomes drool," say the Burundi.) They are not riveting speakers, and they try out rhetorical flourishes only timidly, but both tower over their audiences as tribunes. In a refreshing break with other American public figures, Obama would mostly appear alone before the crowd—not flanked by the usual Politburo of sententious sidekicks.

How strange, I thought, that these two men continents apart and with more than forty years in age difference could sound so much alike.

What are the parallels and the differences between them? There's a physical likeness, certainly. Both Mandela and Obama are *thin* men. They move like natural athletes—Mandela was a boxer in his youth; Obama, apparently, an above average basketball player. Watch how Mandela, even in old age, used to rock a few dance steps on stage and how Obama, during the horrifyingly endless and fatuous presidential campaign, would skip up to the podium. (For how long do American presidents actually govern? Two out of every four years are taken up by stumping.)

And they are conscious of their appearance. The shape is trim, the clothes sharp without being exhibitionist. Mandela has an edge with his patterned "Madiba shirts"; Obama favors the severe apparel of American male seriousness, the drab garb of the power bird with just the tie as a tail feather of color. (These suits are all the more lugubrious when you see phalanxes of bankers, senators, influence peddlers, presidential aides, and other conmen clothed in respectability while lying through their teeth.)

One is tempted to note similarities with other elegant politicians or masters of rhythm—Malcolm X, Patrice Lumumba, Osama bin Laden, Subcommandante Marcos, Max Roach, Maurice Bishop, Robert Sobukwe, Modiba Keita ... Can there be a correlation between the silhouette and the sense of calling? They are of the race of *kings* in the archaic sense, natural leaders who would stand head and shoulders above lackeys and adversaries, radiating resolve and composure. Not for them the vulgar dead-duck strut of a Shoe Bush, the pigeon-toed silkiness of a François Mitterrand, the stagger and stump of a drunken Yeltsin or the torturer-on-home-leave swagger of a Putin, nor the decadent and roly-poly joviality of a Sihanouk. "To enter the dance you have to know how to dance," a Cameroonian saying has it. And (or but): A West Indian maxim warns, "Eggs should not enter the dance of the stones."

They have the bearing of men convinced of higher responsibilities, and this puts them slightly apart from their entourage. They may appear distant but are not unapproachable. In repose their mouths are sad. Bitter even, as of those who have known darkness. And yet, one detects an impish sense of humor never far away. Suddenly the smile is there, unforced, as if from nowhere—generous and bright. "The mouth does not know of Sundays," it is said in the West Indies.

In fact, they give the impression of using themselves to the best effect, of having mastered timing, of being inhabited by faith in a bigger cause but also superbly self-contained. (Obama's campaign was a masterpiece of controlling time despite pressures from ally and foe, to the ultimate buildup cresting in triumph.)

When necessary, outrage can be effectively voiced. I still remember the dressing-down Mandela gave F. W. de Klerk—at that point president of the white minority government in South Africa—when the latter questioned the African National Congress's right to take part in the constitutional negotiations that would lead to the demise of Apartheid and a passing of power. Suddenly Mandela stood very tall as he spoke from the fist to berate the obtuse white leader. No more pretense at fastidious etiquette or civilities; the real issues of moral legitimacy were laid out on the table for all to see. He must have been genuinely angry, but at no moment did one sense a loss of control or direction.

These are men who step delicately but with a clear sense of destination. ("If the foot is not held in check, it will drown its master," the Fulani say.) It must come from knowing how powerfully entrenched the enemy forces are. After all, as stated in Hausa: "Who better than the fish knows the number of teeth in a crocodile's mouth?" Attitude matters. Mandela always demanded respect from his jailers. To turn oneself into a tool presumes an inordinate depth of self-knowledge; to use that knowledge judiciously is to remember the West Indian wisdom: "Before crossing the river, don't insult the alligator's mother."

We know that they both worked on themselves at great length. Mandela has claimed that his first victory was over himself. He entered prison a firebrand and a radical black nationalist; as young political leader he vehemently opposed collaboration with parties from other ethnic groups even if these were on the same side of the divide. As a descendant of royalty, he was also imbued with the historical task of leading his own people, the Xhosa, to freedom from colonial oppression. And then, during the endless years of incarceration on a barren prison island, with the sun like salt in his eyes, he must have explored

the labyrinth of fear and doubt to challenge his own anger and prejudice, however justified it seemed. It was there that the national leader,
the nation builder, was forged. ("It is with the body's water that one
draws water from the well," goes a Housa saying.)

Similarly Obama. According to his memoir *Dreams from My Father*,
he constructed his identity through a willed identification with others,
particularly the African-American community. In the process, he too
had to channel his anger against a perceived impotence and calibrate
his need to belong and be liked. It could only have been a conscious
and deliberate effort. He writes in that book that "to be black was to be
the beneficiary of a great inheritance, a special destiny, glorious burdens that only we were strong enough to bear ... Burdens we were to
carry with style."

("However fearful a man may be, his buttocks will always be behind him," note the Fulani.)

While on the subject: I felt it entirely inappropriate during the campaign that John McCain should be referred to as a "hero" for having been
a gleeful killer and then an admirably brave prisoner of war—presumably
with the inference that Obama is not. To my mind for Obama to have
constructed the life he did, given the odds of his personal background
and the dead weight of centuries of institutionalized racism with its cor-
ollary of self-hate, and to have done so with intelligence and sensitivity
and integrity and grace—now there is true heroism!

Obama's book is powerful and so well written that I'd suggest he's
wasting his talents as president of the USA. Mandela's autobiography,
A Long Walk to Freedom, was clearly ghosted (ironically, the French
term for "ghost writer" is *nègre*), but we're told that Obama wrote his
own. The writerly flourishes and finds are engrossing; at the same
time, I could not but notice the tricks—the unlikely reconstruction of

childhood conversations, the choice in what was to be remembered, the didactic thrust of the text to make of it an exemplary pilgrim's progress.

Who are these composite figures really? The odd thing is that both men can be considered outsiders despite their gregarious, easy and non-elitist ways, and their strong engagement in community affairs despite, also, the obvious adulation they enjoy.

The king, in history, is a lonely posting endowed with supernatural attributes and saddled with more than human responsibilities. The king embodies expectations. People have a *need* to identify with their idol; so that idealization promptly becomes appropriation—and just as ritually he may be sacrificed to placate the gods (presumably also the golden calf on Wall Street) so as to ensure rain and ample crops. Besides, a Bantu saying claims, "Authority, like the skin of the lion and the leopard, is full of holes."

Certainly, these two men seem not to be accepted unquestioningly by the communities they emerged from. They are too singular, suspected of being tainted by too close a frequentation with white. Yet by the very non-belonging/belonging they have opened new tracks of reflection on racial identity and cultural conditionality. Does this mean that they are too "different" to be connected to ordinary folks? Quite the contrary, I'd argue. One only has to see the way they interact with children, going down to look them in the eye with frankness and asking them straightforward and sensible questions, to gauge the extent of their guilelessness.

There are noticeable silences in both their lives, maybe in exact proportion to their very public and apparently transparent presence. Could it be because they are self-made, self-invented? The developing trajectory of Nelson Mandela's life, when he would have been seen to grow to political and public maturity, is forever sealed in obscurity. No one knows what he might have done and become had he followed a "normal" career. By the time he came out into daylight, squinting and smiling he was already an old man, and while still a forceful presence he was doomed to be snared in a web of careerists who had been talking a revolution (let alone the ethics of liberation) they probably never truly imagined or intended to accomplish. Barack Obama, on the other hand, is only at the beginning of his full potential as political beast. He will almost certainly change and be changed by the exercise of power. Once you've sent your first batch of young men to be killed ... His hands will be stained with blood. How can it be otherwise? "The killing of man by man is one of the most ancient habits of our singular species, like procreation or dreams," wrote Jorge Luis Borges.

And of course, the deeply seated ambitions and the sometimes conflicting interests of those who surround him will also labor (and undermine) his territory.

Every man (and woman) is an invention of self. The construct is this perceived product or result we vulgarly know as *identity*. Perhaps the relationship to the father played a role in their definition. There is, after all, a shared African root. In both instances, to varying degrees, the father as domestic figure of authority is absent and needs to be reconstructed if not invented. What is legitimacy without the father? Growing up without one makes for a complex relationship with authority. It also means that you have to be your own father, or the "father" as conceived of by your community.

In Mandela's traditionalist environment the maternal uncle would normally have been the shaping influence. It is told that Rolihlahla Mandela (Rolihlahla—"someone who shakes the branches," in other words, a troublemaker) was entrusted by his father to Paramount Chief Jongintaba. Chief Jongintaba fed him, had him initiated, and gave him his first suit of clothes. Peter Davis, a Canadian filmmaker who researched Mandela's early life for the purposes of a documentary, describes how he came across an unpublished photo of the future leader at about age eighteen, almost certainly wearing the suit given to him by Chief Jongintaba. "It is the portrait of a young man of astonishing self-composure, someone completely sure of himself and of his right to be in this world." Davis then describes how Mandela was so self-assured that he squandered the very rare opportunity of attending Fort Hare University on a point of conscience, and was duly expelled. Chief Jongintaba ordered him to apologize; he not only refused, but also fled the Big House in order to avoid marrying the woman the chief had chosen for him. To finance his flight he stole and sold one of his royal tutor's cattle.

Obama's account of his own life is, similarly, replete with questions about the authority of the father, the absent presence of the father, the role and the lessons of this father whom he calls the Old Man. And what comes through clearly, maybe far more so than in the case of Mandela, is the mother's guiding and formative influence.

Neither Mandela nor Obama can be said to be products of a political machine. From a young age they seem to be poised for striking out on a phased course for leadership. Maybe the combination of uncertainty and pride and anger and empathy and commitment gave them no choice. "He who suffers from diarrhea does not fear the night," holds a Mossi wisdom. At a crucial moment in history they appear to incarnate a huge expectation and desire for change. The despair and disgust with the dispensation imposed by fascist rulers is so prevalent, the desire for change so deep and so urgent that "victory" is inevitable. Men like Mandela and Obama do not engineer the change; they give a face to it, and this change wants to be radical and cathartic.

Can they lead the break? Do they have enough power? Do they not expend the essential of their potential by merely getting into office and on the historical effort of accompanying the paradigm-shattering changes?

The dog has caught the bus—and now what? Are these leaders revolutionaries? Or even visionaries? The moment of taking power may also mark the onset of political impotence. Will Obama be obliged to govern from the center, as Mandela did? Was that not the condition for their coming to power? Out of necessity they gather around them executives who in the final analysis do not accept their ascendancy, or, when they do, will "elevate" (confine) these charismatic leaders to the pedestal of symbols. This is not immediately apparent. Many lips are busy paying service. "You catch a bull by its horns, a man by his words," is a Bantu saying.

And they make cardinal mistakes, for whatever reason but mostly because they want to be seen to be as tough and pragmatic as an ideal father—the father neither of them really knew—would have been. When Mandela acceded to the post of president, he not only decided (was prevailed upon to decide) to preserve South Africa's position as arms manufacturer for the continent, producing military hardware so ideally suited for the bush wars African armies wage on their populations; he also condoned the obscene spree of sophisticated arms acquisition (fighter planes, corvettes, submarines—none of which could be of rational use, and after a while there is no longer the know-how to man the equipment) that would rip the moral guts out of the African National Congress in power.

For Obama these are early days. But already the tests are upon him. "I promise you: as a people we will get there," he declared in his victory speech with a resolute jaw, and people wept. But what and where is the *there* referred to? Is he suggesting that America will regain its predominant position in the world? To do what? To impose military domination in order to protect economic control in order to advance the interests of Halliburton and Blackwater—because military power generates economic activity? Or is he thinking of "that shining city on the hill" that Ms. Palin looked to? And what does *that* consist of other than President Reagan's mausoleum?

Will he allow the crimes committed against humanity (including American humanity) by his predecessor's administration to be brought to book? Will he draw commonsense conclusions from the fact that the financial system—for that matter, the entire globalization project—cannot be "fixed," since it is now clear that unchecked greed and the frenzy of speculation and debt unrelated to real productivity will drag down the whole world? And what will that system be replaced by? Will he—can he—inflect the peculiar American culture posited on the notion that it has the *right* to impose its violence on the world? Already, Obama seems to have ducked the first foreign challenge of real ethical implications, offering no leadership while America's client state Israel is ethnically cleansing Gaza viciously, bloodily, repulsively, and with the impunity of "heroes" shooting fish in a barrel.

Are Mandela and Obama tragic figures who can't possibly live up to mankind's exaggerated expectations? However different they may be from those around them because of their destinies, surely they are only human, and politicians at that, which means that they are expressing a constrained and specific evolution of humanity. "If the nose didn't have nostrils, how would you blow it?" This is a Toucouleur saying.

With cosmic 'luck' and application—for it is a *discipline*—Obama may get to the point where he realizes part of the secret of Mandela's moral longevity: a shedding of the self, that is, that the only way to be replenished is to give. But does this make for feasible politics, that "art of the possible?"

As I approach the last paragraphs of this essay, I'm driving through the dark streets of Dakar after arriving at the chaotic airport on a flight from Paris. Ka'afir, the Senegalese colleague who comes to fetch me and I do a quick roundup of world news since we last met. He brings me up to speed on the latest disappointments caused by the corrupt and inept Wade government: civil servant salaries not paid in two months, power outages lasting days in the poorer neighborhoods, schools on strike, the impossible dearness of basic food, the Lions (Senegal's national football team) not making the cut for the Africa Cup ...

We pause to reflect on all of this. Then he suddenly says, "But the American people gave a lesson in democracy to the whole world."

How so, I ask?

"Obama."

He says nobody in Africa believed that the Americans could find in their hearts the maturity and the fairness to elect a black man to the highest office. I warn that the proof is still to come, that the man may fail because the challenges are too overwhelming, because the people around him have too powerfully entrenched views and strategies different from his (I mention the Israel conundrum).

"Even so," Ka'afir says, "even if he fails, which is likely, the historic fact still remains that the American people grew beyond their fears and prejudices. Their hearts expanded."

Four

IMAGINING AFRICA

In this month of July 2005, two images haunt me. They are not related and perhaps they only gesture indirectly toward issues looming
large in the contemporary world we inhabit—barbarism, terrorism,
imperialism, impoverishment, plagues, the absence of ethical codes
and a hierarchy of values, mad materialism, intellectual and artistic
narcissism ... Yet, both of these images illustrate to me the raw fault
line where "private" and "public" meet.

The first is that of the so-called Piano Man. On the stormy night
of April 7, a young white male is found wandering the streets along the
beach of Sheerness in Kent. His elegant dark suit is soaked, all nametags
have been carefully removed, he has no papers. Apparently he has also
lost his memory and, with that, his identity. If you forget how others
saw you, you no longer exist. The man is taken to the Medway Mari-
time Hospital. The National Centre for Disappeared Persons is alerted.
Nobody comes forward to claim him. Over the next weeks there will be
thousands of reactions, speculations, theories, and false identifications
aired over the Internet, all to no avail (the Web is a vast echo chamber
for the deluded and the conspiratorial), and then interest will subside.

The man is traumatized by fear: when someone enters the room where he is kept he cowers in a corner. After a few days he draws a concert piano on a sheet of paper. He is taken to a grand piano, sits down, and starts playing exquisitely for hours on end. Only while playing does he relax. The blonde young alien with the melancholic and fearful eyes responds to no question, seems not to know any language, draws or writes nothing else, but composes music; he is obviously an accomplished concert pianist and has to be torn away from the instrument. He clutches the folder with his compositions to his chest.

The second image arises or rather tumbles from the sky like some Icarus with burned wings. A severed human leg falls on the roof of the house of Pam Hearne who lives about 9 kilometers from JFK Airport in New York. After landing, further limbs and crushed body parts will be found in the landing gear space of a South African Airways flight from Johannesburg with stopover in Dakar. Again, no nametags and no identity papers. Pam Hearne says she at first thought the noise was caused by a neighbor loading his truck nearby. "I'm glad I live where I live so that I didn't have to run for my life as that man apparently did," she declares. And the authorities announce: "At no stage was there any danger for the passengers on board."

(And since writing the above paragraph, I saw on the Arte television channel a report about one Solomon from the Cameroon who similarly fell from heaven into a maize field in Germany near the Swiss border. It would appear that he did succeed once before, stowing away in the landing carriage of a flight from Douala to Paris. He was fifteen years old, it left him with a perforated eardrum, some fingertips were frozen white and withered and had to be amputated. After a few months he is repatriated to his homeland. Two weeks later he tries again—but this time his iced black body is found among the stalks of a withered maize patch. As the wheels were let down for landing he must have been ejected. Maybe he was already dead then. A jacket and a half-eaten banana are found in his hiding place. In his wallet there's a letter in which he announces his own imminent death as "a fallen angel"; also two photos of Diana and one of Madonna with naked tits. At home the family weeps. He had been buried in the small German cemetery according to Catholic rites. A friend of the family, a Cameroonian woman who often travels abroad, is dispatched to bring back some soil from this grave. She does so, first pleading with the spirit of Solomon not to harm her for thus fetching him to his own. In the home village, the small container of dark German soil is ceremoniously buried in the red earth, strewn over a bed of banana leaves. And now the mother can at last break down and beat her breasts. (Bodies move violently in anguish.)

It is fair to say there has been deterioration in the international environment, both physical and moral. All along the bright thread of human consciousness there exists an awareness of the deleterious implications for groups of the human family when differences are settled through conflict, and concomitantly there seems always to have been a valorization of the search for peace—for attenuating tensions, for moderation and compromise, for codifying justice so that conflicting interests could be settled in accepted ways to obviate the futility of bloodletting. But "peace" is only the temporary suspension of violence. These precious, rare moments along our trajectory ought to be remembered and commemorated, taken down to be dusted off and prayed to. "Moments of peace" ought to be given names and faces so that we may picture them on the home altar and honor them with sacrificial gifts of whiskey and cigarettes and oranges.

Our desire for a solution—for "understanding," for "a way forward"—is insatiable. The pressure we exert for feeling good about ourselves and useful to the suffering masses is a fundamental one—if not fundamentalist.

Without going into man's never-ending propensity and predilection for making war, and thus without any pretense at understanding why this "way of life" appears to be fatal and inevitable (if killing one's neighbor could be described as a way of life), and thus also without daring to assess the viability of age-old countermovements toward pacification—I think it is clear and reasonable to argue that over the last decade or two we have seen an increase in collective killing and a growing numbness to its implications.

The "world"—significant sectors of it at least—objected to black people in South Africa being killed and oppressed just because they were black, and we supported the struggle for justice. Could we say there was as much outrage when genocide took place in Rwanda ten years ago? Are we similarly concerned about what happened in Sierra Leone, Liberia, and Somalia, about what is being done today to people in Darfur and in Zimbabwe and in the Congo, or the threatened mass killings in Côte d'Ivoire—and are we as engaged in trying to prevent these conflicts? Why not? Because these are faraway places with little impact on the equilibrium of forces in the world and have scant market value? Because the killing and oppression are not being done by whites? Or is the issue too complicated, the culture too "dark"? Are we just tired of trying to understand? Have we removed our moral nametags and the memory of who we are, as we play existential tunes on the piano?

We are stalked by an upsurge in fundamentalism on all sides, a rebirth of religiosity, and the imposition of world capitalism as vector of progress, a deepening of poverty and inequality and the return of racism, the decay of common sense and ethics by political correctness. (Did it ever leave? "Fundamentalism" is wily. Depending on the time and the locale it is more or less vocal, more or less obviously foul-smelling.) The United States has become a rogue entity, Europe has gotten as tight as a clay-ox's arse (I'm using an Afrikaans expression) and in Africa the mind is driven mad by misery—our freedoms whittled away in the arbitrary acts of abject rulers or by the unfettered greed of the elites and the exactions of the military plundering the people, and in some places no freedom exists because there are no economic and political means to construct it. Is it then not understandable that desperate individuals will try and escape in frail, overcrowded *cayucos*, or stow away in the landing sections of aircraft where they have no chance of survival because they will either freeze to death or be crunched to a pulp?

What are we to make of the resurgence of cannibalism, of children being given guns to go and kill? How did we, collectively, come to the point where we accept the notion of "failed states," of "black holes"—at least to the point where we seem to be able to live with it? When did we lose the intimate knowledge that what is done or allowed to be done to the defenseless concerns all of us, that the bells toll for us all? And that implicitly condoning the unacceptable is rotting the fiber of our ethical concerns so that we *all* become more brutalized—indeed, less civilized? Have we lost the sense that real change depends on each of us? How did this shift in priorities and balance from the Other to the Self become so all-invasive? We're living in the Age of Entitlement.

True, much of our internationalist concern may have been built on fragile agreements, hypocritical and informed by national or market interests—but, at least, they constituted certain benchmarks and embodied given attitudes defining our conduct in this world. The fact that the superpower is now intervening unilaterally wherever it may deem fit—and so clearly and brutally for its own interests, in the process demeaning the value of human life and the respect for non-Western cultures—has precipitated the destruction of our frail international agreements and attempts at living together in a modicum of peace. Should we then be surprised at the bombs going off in Madrid and London and Bali?

◆

What are the values of the world? In a recent interview, James Wolfensohn, previous president of the World Bank, pointed out that $900 billion of annual global spending by world governments go for defense, $300 billion for supporting or rather subsidizing the world's richest farmers, and only $56 billion for development assistance to the poor. It is a question of investment. Reducing the numbers of the poor, obviously, is not as profitable as promoting the proliferation of arms. Similarly, the media reported that President Bush's "space shield" would cost an estimated $58 billion, whereas experts tracing the implementation of promises also calculate that the announced Millennium Development Goals (reducing poverty significantly by 2015, etc.), as fixed in common and solemn accord by a concert of nearly all the nations, can now only be reached in the year 2147.

This arrogance should be seen against the backdrop of some comparative figures: In 2003 there were 704 million people living in Africa, 307 million in the Euro zone; life expectancy in Africa was 45.6 years on average, 78.9 years in Europe; HIV/AIDS affected 7.2 percent of Africans, in Europe it was 0.3 percent; 457 kilowatts of electricity were used per person in Africa, in Europe it was 5,912 kilowatts; the average yearly income in Africa was $500, in Europe $22,810; 13 percent of the roads in Africa were passable, in Europe it was 95 percent; during that year there were 348,000 airline flights over Africa, in Europe it was 3.5 million. Between 1981 and 2003 the number of people in Africa living on less than a dollar a day rose from 40 percent to 50 percent, in China over the same period it fell from 60 percent to 20 percent. NEPAD (the New Economic Partnership for African Development) budgeted $64 billion annually for the development of Africa's degraded and often inappropriate infrastructure, but over the past four years just one percent has been committed to infrastructure projects.

◆

Indeed, Africa is now poorer than it's ever been. Extreme poverty has multiplied fourfold over the last two decades. More than a third of the continent's inhabitants eke out an existence on less than half a dollar a day. More "development money" has gone into Africa than the Marshall Plan brought to a war-destroyed Europe (although much "African" money returns to the pockets of the donor agencies or their national companies)—and where are our industries, universities, public institutions, hospitals, roads? Our civil wars—such as those in the two most populous states, Sudan and the Congo—have gone on for so long that they seem to be endemic, permanent, and insoluble. An average Nigerian, despite the oil bonanza, is now poorer than in 1970; the country is racked by ethnic and religious disputes and is one of the most corrupt places on earth; the justice system has all but collapsed; civil disorder and capital flight are the norm and the once-proud universities have imploded.

Yes, we still live by profound humanist traditions; and *yes,* on no other continent do people kill people as easily and from as young an age. *Yes,* many of the horrors can be laid at the door of vampire-like leaders, the predators who reduced their populations to bankruptcy and ruin and starvation—Idi Amin, Bokassa, Mobutu, Eyadema, Charles Taylor, arap Moi, Robert Mugabe, Dos Santos ... But *yes*, we must ask as well, what did those who were not personally greedy, the "Christian gentlemen" like Kaunda and Nyerere bequeath other than crazy and ruinous economic policies? The late Claude Aké once said: "It is not so much that development has failed as that it was never on the agenda in the first place."

(And then I need to qualify this unremittingly bleak depiction: Julius Nyerere, at least, seems to have been a brave and creative guiding force, an inspired *mwalimu* (teacher). He will be remembered for the Arusha Declaration that created a code of ethics for public officials, for the resources he poured into education so that the level of literacy was raised to more than 80 percent, for his consistent resistance to pressures from the West. "For us to start making 'claims' on each other's territory would be to play into the hands of those who wish to keep Africa weak, and it might well lead us to the tragic absurdity of spending money on armaments while our people die for want of medical attention or starve from want of knowledge." He even relinquished power voluntarily. Ah, where have our leaders gone?)

For I want to underline in passing that I do not consider Africa's poverty simply to be the fate of a globally unjust system. Part of the cause for our backwardness is certainly systemic—what else can we expect in a world capitalist set-up? But whether we continue to wallow in our poverty, in our self-pitying attitude, depends entirely on ourselves. Africa is not poor. And even though the corrupters may be doing so from London and Paris and Washington, the accomplices and often the beneficiaries are those in Africa who fatten themselves on the misery of the poor. Nobody will or even can save and redress Africa but

the Africans themselves. This is the imperative of wanting to help ourselves, of no longer hiding behind the excuses of "custom" and "culture," of developing a shared sense of the common good, of no longer
living for today's spoils or the meager striving for survival only.

◆

To be creative, we must be freed from attachments. We have to un-
shackle the mind and keep it liberated if we want to stay it from reverting to the darkness of despair and self-interest only. How can the
mind be kept free? It is not enough to sing the darkness. To survive,
we must assume the responsibility of imagining the world differently.
If not, what horizon do we have to offer to a thirteen-year-old boy
in Monrovia who now thinks his only passage to adulthood can be
through acquiring an AK-47, drugging himself, making up his face
with cheap lipstick, donning a wig and some sad imitation wedding
dress, and then going out to kill? What is it that we propose to the
children? What can they live *for*? Not everybody can be a Piano Man.

There is interconnectedness in the world and Africa is part of the
equation, even if that is not where the front line between West and East
is burning. And Africa has always been conceived of both from abroad
and within mostly as an exercise in escapism. It is happening even now:
on the one hand we have a drumming up of support for the continent
through rock concerts and G8 meetings and the establishment of Com-
missions and of Goals; on the other we hear the equally self-serving
mantras of "sovereignty," of the world *owing* Africa a decent existence,
to be based on the reinforcement of all the falsehoods we have come to
know in terms of governance and statecraft and political dispensations,
from colonialism to post-independence.

Historical processes define the North-South relationship, by perceptions and by power equations. Two components that interest me are ethics and power—more precisely, how *non-power* (or imagination) can be used as transformative agent.

Underlying the history of attitudes pertaining to Africa—an up-and-down history with more down than up, a give-and-take story with a lot more taking than there ever was giving—underlying it, there are real cultural differences. Among these, I think, are a shading in approaches to the event and the meaning of death, to notions of continuity from generation to generation and even to the telling of time, differences in ways sentient life feeds into the unknown, in the uses and the sense of body, differences in traditions of bringing the power of darkness to light through rhythm and incantation. The "darkness" I refer to could be seen as a fatalistic given, the obscured world, which instills fear and awe, but also as the source of magic and exorcism. We all celebrate life in order to allay death; in many parts of our dark world we also honor death so as to make life bearable.

◆

These reflections were inspired by an exhibition of African art I recently saw in Paris. It was called Africa ReMix—a terrible name, by the way, as it suggests that one could take some old expressions and shake them up in a new combination!

What struck me in that show was the often direct and bold vitality of expressions, an awareness of the texture of materials and surfaces, and the uses of derision. There was a noticeable mixing of what could be considered "traditional" in the African context—soil, cloth, body art, the appeals to magic—with Western forms and expressions such as installations and video art. The installations often gestured at a narrative intention (we are nothing if we cannot tell ourselves); the video art (as nearly all over the world) was mostly banal and ugly and empty: forms of presentation finding their fleeting and flitting justification only in the museum environment of so-called globalized materialism and demeaned aesthetics as opposed to the more humanist interaction one would have found in customary settings. In other words, this was by and large art made for the Western museum visitor. To be sure, some present-day African "specificity" was bestowed by working with the reject leftovers of consumer societies—tin, old firearms, plastic containers, recycled images—making the wry point that Africa both lives from the discarded scraps of the developed world and that anything, however humble, can be transformed into art.

But beyond this hybridism—most of the African artists represented actually live and work in Europe—uncomfortable questions are posed. Why were these artists grouped? What do artists from North Africa and, say, the Congo have in common? What is it that Africa shares that makes it collectively different from the rest of the world? (I would suggest that one subject of any future collaboration between institutions of the North and the South ought to be a study of the similarities and the differences among artists on the African continent, and between them and the rest of the world.) And why would there seem to be a need from "outside" to see Africa as a whole? Can it be to confirm stereotypes, the updated manifestations of exoticism now coming under the heading of "showing respect for the foreign?"—when the implication is that it is reassuring to keep the continent adrift and exotic but separate in its "foreignness"? (Naturally, the politically corrupt rulers of African countries find it to their advantage to continue promoting this perception of the continent being one and different from the rest of the world.)

Wouldn't it be more pertinent to propose that what is now really "foreign" or "strange" is the way Europe has evolved? Take quintessentially do-good and feel-good countries like Holland and Denmark: the majority of Dutch and Danes are obviously now in revolt against the policies of tolerance and permissiveness and the international solidarity that defined their countries over the last thirty years, and the national face in each instance has become angry, xenophobic, and even racist.

How did this come about?

Apart from the obvious problems, mostly economic, of not being able to absorb large numbers of immigrants, there must surely also be cultural contradictions: excessive tolerance of diversity (in theory) coupled to boundless permissiveness misjudged the need for a sense of national cohesiveness and vocation, even of identity, for it is true that relatively homogeneous cultural groupings do cling to the unchanging familiarity of the geographic areas they inhabit; mixing did not necessarily bring about a greater acceptance of diversity—it was mistakenly assumed that those you accept in their difference would reciprocate by respecting your "otherness" and that thus you'd find shared nonreligious grounds upon which to build together; an over-bearing moralistic approach internationally—and a sort of integrationist attempt to have the poor world adopt what the democrats thought was good for them (like "democracy"!)—took account neither of history nor of the North's own hypocrisies, and it resulted as backlash in the revival of an extreme right in their own backyards; leaning over backward to be politically correct and, in fact, to be multiculturally prescriptive, made it impossible, as well, for them to use common sense and to apply basic commitments to human rights. Shouldn't a human right—such as the inalienable right of a woman not to be a serf under whatever religious yoke, and not to be subject to sexual mutilation—*always* outweigh whatever self-serving and escapist respect there may be for the "cultural specificity" of the other?

◆

Nothing of the above can blur the questions we ought to ask ourselves *within* Africa in order to release a creative and transformative imagination. I know we think that to admit to the horrors—of *our* making, *our* responsibility—is traitorous, since it may well reinforce racist typecasting. The struggle will be betrayed, it is often averred. Also, self-assessment will deprive us of the comfort of being victims of history, of colonialism, of racism, of capitalism, of socialism, of our own innocence and inherent goodness ...

We need to start from the terrible recrimination that recognizes we have descended from liberation euphoria to the heart of darkness. We need to admit that the nation-state concept as existing in Africa at present, accommodating rapacious local elites and corrupt and cynical foreign companies only, is not viable. The democracy that has spread over us, even when sweetened by the poison of elections, is killing us. We need to see that foreign development aid is not helping. We know that Africa has to be founded again on radical new premises, informed by genuine autonomy and independence. We know we need a revolution in ethics, in commitment to the needs of the continent, in paring back our inflated rhetoric and our demagogic posturing. And this is neither the task nor the responsibility nor even within the ambit of the moral awareness of the world out there. They, out there, can only think it is anyway not in their interest.

I would postulate that we of this generation suffer from a massive failure of moral imagination. Instead of responsible freedom

we substituted self-enrichment and entitlement linked to cowardice, bad faith, the corruption of dependence, and that glorification
of impotence or of posturing expressed as political correctness, where
our languages were gutted of texture and color and we posited our
shrill interventions on the mumbo jumbo of "healing" and "closure,"
changing the terms we use for looking at the objectionable in the hope
of thus repressing horrible realities. In some instances, we even went
through the sinister farce—or are still indulging in it—where "con-
fessing" to torture and repression is intended to lead to an absolution
supposed to bring about "reconciliation." This must be a prime example of practicing the hypocrisy of religiously motivated "contrition"
as snake oil for social leprosy in order not to lose the essential: the
power and the privileges of the rich and those whom they co-opt.
Anything, any show, any stuffed bird—but the firm commitment to
proceed from our shared humanity to identify what is unacceptable
and to bring about justice!

◆

What if our artists and intellectuals satisfy themselves with ironic
commentary, as in Africa ReMix? What if they are only saving their
own skins, wallowing in a cult of victimization, shifting the blame,
going into ever-denser labyrinths of pursuing the alienated ego?
Then who would speak up and cry? Who would practice the rigors of
the free mind?

As I walked out of the Africa ReMix show I saw an elderly white
man, modishly dressed in a dark suit over a black T-shirt emblazoned
with red letters saying: "Africa is burning." And I wondered whether
we are to be reduced to a fashionable T-shirt slogan.

◆

Freedom is guilt, because it brings with it the knowledge of unfreedom. You could also say: Freedom is awareness, and thus responsibility.

I believe it is possible to have interaction between South and North where there will be conscious efforts made to strengthen one another—informed by full frankness but also based on absolute equality. What Europe does for Africa, Africa must be able to respond to in kind. I believe such interaction should favor and promote *movement*; that it should deliberately set out to bring about *spaces* of creativity, contestation, and transformation (in both directions) and thus be privileging the strengthening of *individuals*. I believe we should practice non-power (in both directions) by refusing to shore up the credibility and the supposed sovereignty of corrupt regimes living off theft and repression and protocol and appearance, and by equally refusing to accept the globalization of free-market systems that are killing the weak.

The imagination I'm talking about must be shaped. From where I'm speaking, we know what some of the answers may look like. We know this involves working in *partnership* with others—NGOs, international bodies, donors—so that, through building the necessary research background and strengthening the means to understand the causes of conflict and the levers of development, and through establishing networks, we may mobilize *expertise*. It will mean that we should be continuously looking for ways of forging *tools* that can be used by others as well, for creating *models* that may be exemplary, and that we are guided by a rigorous *assessment* of the *impact* of what we do. As we are condemned to the pursuit of excellence, nourished by the equilibrium between reflection and action, we will always want to be *innovative*, to "think out of the box."

Questioning all assumptions of legitimacy and "historical truth," or the glib justifications of nation-building and purported majority rule must shape the new horizon we propose; it cannot afford to succumb to the dictates of the lowest common denominator. In art, ethical clarity (which is not the same as certainty) is the prerequisite for keeping our tools sharp and effective. It is also our specific expression of solidarity with all those who are oppressed. As cultural practitioners we just cannot afford to assume that the market ideology must shape the outlines of our imagination. All of the above implies an ongoing awareness of the nature of responsive and accountable consciousness.

To put it in a broader context: We know that essential contributions to peace building, to development, to the reshaping of Africa—will be made by organizations of women and of the youth, by those active in cultural creativeness, by all those who can engage the roving armed bands of feral boys and girls on questions of formation for citizenship, by motivating our interventions with thorough and exact knowledge and on an ongoing search for understanding the reasons for communal tensions and the ways out, by revalorizing the role played by traditional structures and indigenous methods in matters of conflict mediation and survival—and all of the above premised on understanding and exploring the links between imagination and creation.

For I believe that it *is* possible to strengthen and season the freedom of the mind, singly and collectively, and that this freedom constitutes the necessary lever for bringing about further changes.

◆

P.S. *Of course, it needs to be pointed out that the Piano Man, after the febrile speculations died down, turned out to be a waiter from Bavaria—*

scorned in his love for another man, mortified by the difficulties of living. Apparently, he studied the behavior of amnesiacs and then set out on his quest for reinventing himself in accordance with a romantic dream. There are not many ways to escape from this world of control and cataloguing anymore ... And for us, this unexplained apparition—from the sea in the dark as if from outer space, and I had to think of Dino Buzzati's haunting short story, "The K."—was endlessly intriguing, reaching down into our watery memory of being the total stranger, the child abandoned at birth or suckled by wolves, the angel.

There are not many ways to escape from this world ... Year after year, despite accrued patrolling by Spanish and Italian armed forces along the coasts of Africa to try and intercept them, despite the criminalization of thousands among those who make it to Europe by keeping them in "retention camps" or by relegating them to the status of shadowy fugitives, more and more gray-faced people in tattered clothes literally risk their lives in trying to "get to paradise." "Europe or death!" is the cry going up. Among them are women and children. These are the first to die, sometimes thrown overboard, the anonymous bodies rolling in the surf, washing up on beaches where tourists sun themselves.

Five

THE AFRIKANER AS AFRICAN

When it was hot, Charles van Onselen and I stood in the swimming pool outside the conference hotel with emerald water up to our waists and decided we were getting too old for farting with fools, too dulled to be angered by anything, particularly the posturing of bad faith presented as intellectual discourse in the meeting room from which we had just now escaped. Nothing to be deplored though, for to fight would have been senseless and brought along heart palpitations. One might have been tempted to pick up rocks and smash skulls, and that can be terribly exhausting. Besides, of what help would it have been? As Edmond Jabès wrote: *"You are dead. You escape the imagination."* Let's not go there.

Over the parapet around the hotel's grounds we watched the ocean with dhows coming in to port the way they have always done, like giant wooden geese using paddles to walk on the waves, and we wondered what that meant in terms of a preserved sense of time and topography. Exquisite young women of "mixed race" (with what was the human race mixed?), draped from head to hem in black, wove their steps with supple hips through the narrow streets of Stone Town. One ogled slip-per-clad foot peeking out from under a perfumed robe. Earlier, a guide had shown us the inside of the cathedral; he said Livingston's badly embalmed body was kept there before being shipped back to the sods of "home," the sun sometimes has a rotten smell; he also pointed out the tree to which slaves were tied for flogging, and repeated several times in a heavy accent: "Sank God dis sing is over."

Really?

I should note that our fatigue was maybe brought on by a "dark" emotion seeping from deliberations in the place of discussions we'd fled, to wit that the Afrikaners would have to pay reparations to the rest of the continent for the privilege of being accepted, eventually, as *Africans*. It was nearly as if to be African was synonymous with being a victim, and thus endowed with a strange moral superiority, a closed circle to be defended fiercely, no erstwhile devil would be allowed to butt in. Nearly then, as if to be *black* was to be blessed with the "comforts" of a never-ending pain that could not be rationalized: a last sign of difference. It was all very well. Nothing can substitute the pain of the other. But if we were to go down this road and apply these criteria, somebody suggested—how far back do we go and where does the buck of retribution and restitution stop? Were the Afrikaners, apart from being bastards in their own right, not also but the overseers and foremen of international capitalism? Are we, by inference, to condemn our black forefathers for not having successfully resisted exploitation? How can we condone the moral superiority of the victims? What if both perpetrator and victim are black? What do we do, say, about the Hutus? Does their blackness absolve them from responsibility for the atrocities committed? And if not, how do *they* pay back? Are they to spend a penal pause in purgatory, for the time being not admitted to the purity of being Africans?

◆

What goes into composing the concept or presentation we call Afrikaner? Let me not romanticize—we tend to forget now how important notions and theories of "race" were in Europe and America in their justification of Western expansionism. Still, the attempt to identify the Afrikaner, or similarly the African, cannot be based on moral evaluation. Like any other cultural construct the Afrikaner is the product of history (at times other people's histories), and of an evolution in perceptions. Of choices too. And history is singularly cruel and brutal; it is always the sun darkening you. The Afrikaner was successively and sometimes simultaneously victim and destroyer, both oppressor and oppressed. For instance, he fights British imperialism, has his farms torched in a scorched-earth policy and his wife and children starved in concentration camps, only to go on and become a racist and plundering overlord.

The title of my wanderings over the pages that I presented in that room of reproaches ("The Afrikaner as African") may strike you as an oxymoron. After all, semantically speaking, *Afrikaner* is but the translation of the word *African* in Afrikaans. It is possible in the Afrikaans language to distinguish between "Afrikaner"—meaning an Afrikaans-speaking person issued from the whitish African tribe of a special concoction in the southern regions of the continent, however one draws the ethnic outline—and "Afrikaan" as the translation of African, meaning black. In practice the two are seldom used together as a pair of opposites; one hears rather of *Afrikaners* and *Africans*. Maybe Afrikaner and Afrikaan are too close for comfort on one tongue. (And they who dwell on one tongue may get their spittle mixed.)

It is believed the word "Afrikaner" first originated to designate the offspring of mixing between European settlers and functionaries on the one hand (with few women among them), and the indigenous people encountered along the shores around the Cape on the other, particularly their women. It is even thought that some clans grouping these "mixed-blood" descendants took on the generic name of "Afriquas," the suffix -*qua* denoting "son of," and thus in this instance indicating "sons of Africa." I advance these theories conditionally; much more research needs to be done before we may draw certain conclusions.

What can be shown is that, at different moments of mixing, entities split off to form new tribal conglomerations or constellations, often grafted onto remnants of preexisting groupings—thus the Griquas came into being, and later the Basters ("bastards")—horsemen raiders with rippling feathers in their broad-brimmed hats. And thus too, in a process of transformation from dark hand to lighter-hued one, the Afrikaners. "Coloureds" came much later, as a ragbag and arbitrary political signifier forcibly regrouping all the conquered and decimated non-Black indigenous people and those who had willy-nilly been tainted by mixing with white, and bringing with it economic consequences. To this day one will find Cape Coloured families with the surname "Afrikaner."

Another pointer to the origin of the term "Afrikaner," often cited, is when a certain Hendrik Bibault (or Biebouw—the French had already given way to the Dutch) is taken to court for refusing the law of the Dutch East India Company, having ransacked in a drunken roust the Stellenbosch magistrate's office. The Company ("Jan Kompanjie") not only disrupts and ultimately destroys the life-pattern of the Khoi people, not only imports and exploits slaves from its possessions in the East or bartered for elsewhere in Africa, but also rules over the subject functionaries, farmers, and soldiers and even the "free burghers" with a tight Dutch fist. The incident happens early on during the settlement of the trading post, in 1707, and a rebellious Bibault shouts: "Ik ben een Africaander!"

Bibault's defiant cry (I am an Afrikaner!) of secession from Dutch law and company sovereignty must have been a leap toward defining another identity. He says: I am beyond your possession. But he also says: You cannot tax me or govern over me since I'm no longer a Dutchman or a Frenchman; I'm of *this* continent. The general conditions of his environment and his situation now narrow down to a specific attempt at redefinition. An interesting line of exploration would be to understand why, in disaffiliating from the known "racial" and cultural group to which he belongs and in the absence of being able to become part of any other grouping present in his environment, he should choose to become "African." To what extent, if ever, during this shift in self-definition did he recognize the shared Africanness of the Khoi people? For that matter, did the Dutch and other colonials think of the inhabitants of Africa as "Africans" or were they distinguished by tribal connotation? And when did the continent's inhabitants start referring to themselves as Africans? Or was Bibault to be (or become) an "Afrikaner" exactly because he was no longer the one and not yet the other? Caught in a middle world, as it were? Did "Afrikaner" then mean to be the rainbow that is neither sun nor rain but a pretty illusion spanning the two? This African consciousness I'm here referring to, of course manifests itself long before the advent of Pan-Africanism or Africanism.

What changed when he made his leap? Surely not his race. Is change the outcome of evolution, an inescapable process? An act of will? Or just a bad hangover? Does it not also imply a touch of alienation? A glimmer of reality gives alienation so much more meaning ...

One should point out that someone like Bibault evidently had some choice in the matter whereas many others—the so-called Vryswartes

(Free Blacks), the slaves and the political exiles brought to the Cape, those shipwrecked on its reefs, the descendants of mixed unions between settlers and colonized—obviously had no say in the process of becoming "Afrikaners." For a long time it was assumed they had no voice either.

They did, of course, even if history forced their documents and their languages underground. In 1750, the Raja of Tambora, a political "undesirable," writes the entire Koran from memory in the house of Simon van der Stel who, as governor of the Cape was himself of "mixed descent." Slaves or exiles left documents written in Malayu, Sunda, Buganese, and Arabic. An early development is Arabic-Afrikaans: Afrikaans written in Arabic calligraphy. A precursor in this is Jan van Boughies who went to the Cape in 1786 as the slave of Salia of Macassar, herself a former slave.

(A pathetic footnote to the Bibault saga: As troublemaker he is exiled to Australia, presumably Tasmania, where he dies—a lone foreigner among aboriginal strangers.)

◆

The thread (the process—and the threat!) interesting to me, you would have noticed, is that of the Afrikaner as bastard African.

He/she is the hybrid product of long periods of mixing—between Europeans of many kinds (making of him a sort of proto-European), slaves of diverse origins on two continents, and the indigenous peoples. Genealogy and morphology show us this process. The Afrikaans language testifies to it.

The process is obviously not exclusive to the Afrikaners; it echoes experiences of other African tribes and cultural groups. Imagine the various permutations of the Fulani, or think of how Swahili came about as another example.

But it is true that "establishing" any "identity" consciously involves a founding act—or several, repeated and renewed down the ages. With the Afrikaners these moments were mostly represented as "language movements." Usually, the acts would be accompanied by sets of supposed principles and criteria, mostly religious. The way an Afrikaner is defined now is certainly different from when it happened in the past. It started as a self-declaration (up to today it is still, under certain circumstances, a choice—though, more and more, it has become a burden and most of the concerned people now experience it as a shame and whistle as they look the other way, hoping not to be noticed as they skulk through the graveyard), conveying the urge to exclude as well, and even attempting to "purify" or "purge" the tribe. Soon enough there would be laws to protect "the purity of the *race*" concocted by Nazified intellectuals, a purity all the more viciously searched for and enforced as the nature of this "race" was to be, and will always be, the product and the process of mixing.

A first tentative general formulation of this sort of process, then: that identity is predicated upon a mode of perception, how one sees and situates oneself, through what mirror the other is seen, upon the value ascribed to these perceptions, and that it is thus *an act of recognition* presupposing exclusion and demarcation.

From its inception certain attributes could be ascribed to the cultural construct, which—I insist—is largely the result of rupture, of striking out for an interior, of "going into Africa." Not unlike the Tuaregs, that other "white African" tribe, the Afrikaners are instinctive nomads: you could say because they're restless or runaways, because they want to conquer and to tame, but also because they want to be different and apart or simply pioneers and explorers. They need to be on the move as both plunderers and pastoralists.

They carry with them a deep conviction of self (of belief and of destiny) and an equally profound uncertainty: continuously, from the time the umbilical cord was cut with a blunt knife they had to define and purge and situate the collective self. They are in abject awe of that unapproachable Unum God whose buttocks promulgated their farted destiny as a "chosen people," so that they could think of themselves as being pious and not just Sunday shitters—but then they blaspheme against humanity in their acts and their laws. They project themselves as being conservative and yet they are constantly engaged in the art of changing and adaptation. Survival was premised on having "to make different" (*die groot andersmaak*)—actually a metamorphosis. Then, and now again, to survive you had to initiate change and unleash potential.

◆

How is the bastard identity formed, I asked? By mixing, by making other, by painful or pleasurable or shameful passages from the known to the unknown (urgently manifesting its need to become known), by seizing the moments of intervention, by inhabiting niches and exploring interstices, by moving, by traveling deeper, by learning to read the wind, by confrontation, through struggle, and by conflict. The bastard, I think, has a heightened sense of identity-awareness as pathology and as passport, perhaps of the furtiveness thereof: the past is more complex and entangled than that which meets the eye, the future less certain. Identity accrues from the wells and the pastures and the stars along the lines of the journey. It has the smell of blood. *The Afrikaner is only an identity in becoming another.*

The bastard identity that I claim is therefore itself a dialectic with multiple contradictions—looking for certainty, ambivalent about itself, relishing the ambivalence, but changing all the time; having to invent the presence of self, the past, and future as well, by its own moral boot-straps; moving away from the totalizing to the contradictory textures of being alive; creolizing its sense of this mutant self as it moves along the ridges and the edges of change; always facing the process of becoming and the prospect of the unknown, and knowing that all unfolding is upon the unknown—and therefore with a premonitory sense of extinc-tion, of death? Dying will be a certainty.

Even the very thread of consciousness—the language—is in con-stant evolution. One's mother tongue is not just the dimension and the horizon, both praxis and proxy and product and prostitute of personal and communal consciousness. Taking the difficult road of promot-ing mother tongue education, for instance, in the politically correct tyranny of South Africa where "history" is chanted in the histrionic hysteria of breast-beating, will suggest that the potential of language is more than just being the lowest common denominator of communica-tion and record among diverse groups: it is, as well, a tool of inventive-ness and renewal, a voice of history (among many others) and thus the living tissue from past to present, and that all of this must go toward enabling citizens to develop a critical stance to the state. Because your language is also your contact with the inchoate, the prerational, the ut-tering of dawn and the mutterings of dusk, the dark shadows flickering around the meanings of words, the "deeper" sense of existing. Mole-talk is hole-talk. The state's policy on minorities and their languages as markers of their "separate" identities is inevitably a translation of the scope of freedom it will allow its citizens.

◆

Let me digress here. It is about power and formulation ... In early Chinese history, I read, the creation of language was the prerogative of the Son of Heaven. Thus, anyone attempting to create a new one was punished by death. But in a distant part of Hunan province this is exactly what women did centuries ago. "Sworn sisters" forged a language of more than twenty thousand words and at least fifteen hundred characters called Nushu, "female writing," meant exclusively for women, sometimes embroidered on handkerchiefs and fans or other wedding presents for the new bride. It was used to convey the misery of being a female and a wife forced into an arranged marriage and now about to come under the harsh rule of a mother-in-law, a chattel and a slave to the lord, and that later there would be the agony and the blood of childbirth. Life was black and there was strong wind in the branches. One initiated woman with bound feet making shoes or clothes at home would pass on secret knowledge of this ancient way of communication to another by singing it softly, the other would learn by taking the songs to heart and then an oath of silence would bind them together forever. The men probably knew but had nothing but disdain for these "ant characters," these "mosquito scrawls." Were the things pertaining to women not inferior and insignificant? Some even referred to it as "witch's script." Little did they realize that opinions and commentary were being smuggled right under their noses. This discreet tongue, so little known to the outside world, came to light because one of the very last speakers of Nushu, Yang Huanyi, passed away recently at the venerable age of ninety-eight (according to an obituary in the *New York Times* of October 7, 2004). She had mastered the language while still a child and went on to write for others. A kind of sister of mercy, in other words. After two years of marriage a snake bit her first husband and he died. By her second husband who was a gambler, who smoked and laughed and drank with his buddies and who ran up huge debts, she had eight children. The "invisible messages" intended to confidentially comfort and instruct one another could, however, not protect them from the harsh destiny of being woman, nor could it ameliorate their lot. Or did it, emanating as it were from the lap of suffering and bearing the history-blackened traces of patient fingers? And now this language is about to die. What am I saying? It is already dead. (And Edmond Jabès wrote in one of his luminous books: *"The word does not die like a man ... With it the universe crumbles."*)

◆

The spasms, turmoil, and regurgitations of history leave us with devolutions of hyphenated identities. (You could call them thorns in the flesh only too often producing horns.) But paradoxically, there is as well a stronger sense of belonging and of the elements constituting what we call "roots"—place, language, memory, imagination. I imagine the Fulani on the move is more concerned with definition than the sedentary Bambara or Mossi may be. Landscape (the desert?) is a mirror secreting images of self. (*"The intimate tenderness of the desert."* —Edouard Glissant.) In the absence of the founding myths of race, "belonging" (or the need to belong) becomes exacerbated. Hence the importance of the land and a linking agreement called "identity," which is arbitrary and ideological but which will at least remember the land. Hence too, the penchant for religious or ethnic fundamentalism that will at least provide some certainty to fill the void of uncertainty of origins.

The bastard is inevitably a chameleon. He/she is the go-between for perhaps vastly different "parents." The Afrikaner may well bring some African insights to Empire. This go-between function can make of him a facilitator, but it also opens up the possibilities or temptations of double-crossing and the betrayal of others and of self.

Ethics come into the equation. If you "choose" who you are, there's a sharpened sense of finitude, of beginning and ending and of purpose. N. P. Van Wyk Louw—a prominent Afrikaner poet—once famously declared that a people without honor do not have the *right* to exist.

It is against this background, and taking into account the broader implications of ethno-nationalism and the politics of identity, that I look at Fuck-land (South Africa) and the larger continent. Africa—that unblemished wound on universal consciousness—is the "dark forest" of predilection where one takes one's little hand mirror for walkabouts. Feathers blow about the bloodstained yard as you leave the house. Africa is both an exterior and an interior space of mind. Space is important. Equally so light. And wind. There's a reassurance (a resonance) and an excitement in seeing the distant blue horizon constantly on the verge of being erased by the wind of oblivion. Africa is both an elsewhere, the memory of an ancient phantasm, rolling plains with abundant wildlife for the pot, King Solomon's mines, Monomotapa—and the hard, engaging but inescapable destiny of dying, the land where you plant the seeds and mine the minerals and from which you cannot be extracted.

Identification—better, *recognition*—is important to the bastard: this is a spiritual but also a spatial process. It is as well a question of security—you have to be able to identify and situate the potential adversary before he puts a blade through your heart. Maybe the self-chosen African is more acutely aware of the surroundings because these are at the same time reassuring and foreign.

◆

I read the above now—ornate empty thoughts originally written for that presentation to the insufferable meeting in Zanzibar and then worked over again for a subsequent conference in Stuttgart—and I realize it doesn't mean anything to me anymore. At several points in my life the conundrum of a supposed "identity" would be an issue. I'd stand up to be counted as an Afrikaner, claim the identity in order to better subvert tribal orthodoxy from within as it were, denounce and renounce it angrily, be considered a traitor to the people (which I was), defend it against the immensely hypocritical and morally self-serving "superiority" of the English-speaking whites, reclaim it as protest against the equivalences and simplifications of history disguised as the juggernaut of "liberation," try and fight for its bastard essence as a home-grown product of Africa and as acute example of what constitutes the nature of all South Africans in our long history of transformation and of reciprocal change through bloodletting, and for the sake of diversity against the hegemony of commissars and courtesans who have no understanding of the living matter of language and the exulting texture of differences, be courted then by lizards nostalgic for lost power, subsequently to be shat out massively and decisively by "the people" as rabble-roused by opportunist opinion-makers, excommunicated from pulpit and insulted in op-ed articles ...

Until it just didn't matter at all. I'd been playing games a long time. (*"My people, provided that I have one"* —is the way Kafka referred to his fellow Jews.) Actually I'd ceased being an Afrikaner. My sense of that entity, and even of the language, was but nostalgia encapsulated in an irrevocably lost past. Maybe I'd made up that past, coloring it in the

glowing tones of innocence, contextualizing its dark and bleeding violence to make it seem part of the woof of being human.

And now I couldn't be bothered to remember. "I"? What "I"?
The language, if I still used it, had become private and personal. Some
words were left, moving like maggots through the dead meat of redundant arguments. But now I no longer identified in any way. What am I
saying? It is already dead. I was talking of dead people. I am talking of
a passed away "self."

Six

ON "PROGRESS"

I grew up then in a cultural environment still largely shaped by Protestant ethics and distantly influenced by the Enlightenment as if by the *frisson* of a rumor of daring. The world was an ordered place where everybody had his rank and destiny and one's hard work and morally upright behavior were said to contribute toward making it better for everybody who lived in it. Modernity—despite fears evoked by its dangerous premises of greater laxness, like young boys smoking and girls wearing shorter skirts—was believed to lead inexorably to the ongoing development of society. Learning was imperative and considered a prerequisite for the unshackling of potential. Laws of nature could be explained scientifically and every new discovery became a truth pushing back the preceding darkness and superstitions. Were technological advances not deemed to be civilizing factors? Humanitarian values were gaining ever more acceptance, even if fitfully so and subject to qualification and regression in times of crisis. Religious faith and affiliation were increasingly turning into private concerns. In this vale of tears there could be no final spiritual gratification we were told—although social standing was within reach and to be strived for because it would give you bulk and bliss—but one was anyway preparing a shiny place for oneself in the Hereafter. There is something special about the vanity of humbleness. Power was to be used parsimoniously except where there were upstarts not knowing their place, and of these an example was made for the edification of all. Meanwhile, it was becoming acceptable that women should lead independent professional lives. Hair was worn longer and music became louder. Nazism and fascism had been decisively defeated, democracy was on the rise, and there was even talk of going to the moon. It went without saying that mankind was becoming cleverer from one generation to the next. Why, even the sky was no longer the limit!

In short, we were the vectors and the products of *progress* and this Promethean concept was not only a desirable added value to our existential sense of purpose on this earth, but also believed to be the inevitable mainspring for bettering communal life. We all wanted to be progressive; it was thought of as a positive attitude among emancipated people. It helped relax cumbersome sexual mores. Only later did it become suspect as a camouflage for liberalism, if not downright pinkishness and hedonism.

In my situation however, the "progress" I was exposed to translated as paternalistic property, prerogative, and privilege, its applications meaning different things depending on the ethnic group you were ascribed to; it was still hampered by the narrow vision, European values, the outdated beliefs and narrow conservatism and iron taboos of the governing white minority. That is how, later, by then fretting at the tight-mindedness of "my people," I came to subscribe to the liberation ideology of freedom movements so prevalent in colonized countries at the time. Ethnic or religious nationalism for instance, was deemed by correct-thinking progressive people to be an impediment to the emancipation of the downtrodden, and reactionary to boot. A large part of our collective thinking was now informed by historical and materialist determinism. History could be traced in advancing steps with each phase, we just *knew*, heralding a growing consciousness opening onto the development of shared improvements in the state of man. The struggle for freedom was guided by the scientific and ineluctable phenomenon of *progress*. We were going to supersede national boundaries and the redundant demarcations of religiosity. Human life was ever *improving* with the advent of more and more industrialization, easier communication, more generalized transportation, antibiotics, and plastic ... The quintessentially Western concept of "New Man," probably going back to the very early Christian imperative of "conversion"—and thus the possibility to be "reborn" and to strive toward "perfecting" existence—became the bedrock of our utopia. Liberty was on the march. Besides, we knew who the enemy was. We would tear down the structures of iniquity and ill-gotten gain to make way for progress; we would wage war for peace!

Except that I was shortsighted. In due time and through many experiences of having my nose bloodied and my heart made blue, it became clear that there were probably only minimal changes in man's behavior or consciousness over all the ages as far back as our memories or investigations could reach, and that these small variations could be ascribed to specific circumstances, as if to shallow hollows in time modifying the resonance of a tune. They were variations on the themes of self-delusion and barbarism. More: that every "advance" in our shared condition set off a dialectical process whereby we lost as much as we gained, if not more.

The imposition of capital punishment had regressed in most parts of the world (with the notable exceptions of countries like the USA,

China, Iran, and Cuba), and yet we have more officially whitewashed "targeted killings" and random elimination of opponents than ever before. It had been internationally agreed to ban torture (again, with the abstention of the USA—we see the results in the Guantánamo penal colony and the concentration camp of Abu Ghraib), and probably never before have as many people been tormented for the ostensible purpose of "extracting information," but in fact to get them to confess. We believed that the United Nations was an adequate international compromise for federating hope and mediating conflict, and then it was emasculated by the planet's lone superpower because it considered its own interests as paramount, and by the minor despots flaunting their vanity. We were told that Muslims had become more pious, God-fearing, and human loving, and yet the stoning to death of women for supposedly infringing religious rules is now not uncommon. Soon nearly everybody had a car or dreamed of having one, preferably a gas-guzzling SUV—so that suddenly there were a million spurious reasons for clogging roads and streets and even bicycle cities like Beijing and Hanoi became gridlocked and blue with poisonous gases. We all obtained cell phones, and now we are flocks of endlessly chattering sparrows with nothing to say and isolated from one another like deaf quails. We all took to television like fishes to murky water, and now we have hackneyed imaginations infected by continual exposure to lies and to the teasing of desires that can never be satisfied. There were soon no taboos about what we could see in the movies—in the name of our freedom of expression!—and now we are impervious to rape, pedophilia, and the pornography of senseless killing. We all acquired computers, and soon we will have no more capacity for storing and translating memory. We get our news on the Net—and we are inundated by urban myths, gossip, paranoia, and the excesses of unbridled narcissism. We mastered the skies, and now we can inflict impersonal death over long distances. There's a chicken on nearly every plate, and now we're stuffed with hormones and antibiotics. In fact, we abused so much of the miracle cures to combat infectious diseases that our bodies have become all but immune to medication. European farmers are subsidized not to produce crops, and millions of people are starving to death. We grow rich and fat on breeding thousands of pigs, and now we cannot drink the water of the earth because of accumulated nitrates from pigs' piss. We buy and consume to our hearts' delight, and are smothered by detritus and waste. We trash the earth in an orgy of pollution to satisfy our immediate greed. Even the poor have access to hamburgers and fries and fat and sugar and fizzy chemicals, and so we are all becoming obese. We stimulated our economies by producing and selling arms, and now thirteen-year-old killers with wigs and Kalashnikovs each cheaper than a bag of rice have no other way of being initiated into manhood except by running amuck. Through it all ran and runs the golden thread of globalization, the parlor name for crude world capitalist exploitation: we were conditioned to buy and buy and buy, and the poor became poorer.

True, we did "progress," through mobilization supposedly embodying international concern, to the combating of new concepts: ethnic cleansing, genocide, and ethnocide. And then we had Cambodia and Bosnia and Kosovo and Rwanda and Chechnya and Darfur. The West committed itself to exporting democracy by bomb, the kind of democracy that sees evangelical faith and unreason trumping reason and fact-based governance—and we look away from cities flattened to rubble and thousands of civilian deaths. Iraqi resistance fighters bog down the American occupiers, thus probably provisionally saving Iran and Syria from invasion—and then we see them using knives to saw off the heads of innocent hostages in the name of Allah. The Jews were nearly exterminated during the Holocaust, and we have the Israeli state condoned with effective impunity as one of the most ruthless killing and thieving machines of state terrorism. The Palestinians were scattered and driven into exile, and then we witnessed their historical leader, Arafat, as one of the biggest crooks in modern times. (But in the name of solidarity we kept quiet.) Afghanistan was freed of the Taliban, and it is now once again providing 80 percent of the world's heroin. Fidel Castro personified revolutionary fervor and rectitude and stood up to the gringo, and now we know that some of those attempting to flee the socialist paradise will be shot as terrorists and the dissident poets clapped in prison, and his brother will be a godfather to Colombia's drug lords. The Soviet Communist Party is destroyed for all practical purposes when the regime is brought down, and now we have a KGB officer ruling with an iron fist. Europe unites, and the only shared foreign policy it has is to establish an exclusionist fortress.

And what about Africa? (For that is where my heart rots.) Independence was granted or won, and now nearly all African countries depend on international handouts in order to survive while their leaders-for-life plunder and loot the populations. (But in the name of solidarity and because we understand the need for historical *Wiedergutmachung* we keep quiet. We have no shame left.) President Wade of Senegal donates 1.5 million dollars to an American association for training space-age scientists while thousands of infant so-called Talibes (learners) are walking the streets of Dakar with empty begging tins. Algeria fights a heroic struggle to free itself from French colonialism, and then descends into a hell of corruption and fundamentalist violence where thousands are slaughtered like sheep. The majority comes to power in South Africa, and now not all the fat cats are white anymore and some whites join the ranks of the poor blacks who have become poorer and thus ever more driven to criminality. Angola finally brings its vicious civil war to an end, and its president is probably the richest robber alive. Who stuffs his pockets with bribes? Who incites the "legal authorities" to hang the dissenters? Who dictates that aid will only be given if you free up your markets? Who knows what is happening in the interior? Who cares? Eritrea becomes emblematical of self-sufficiency and a homegrown honesty and unpretentiousness, and then the power-sick president wastes thousands of lives in an obscene war with the Ethiopian cousins over a few square miles of arid rocks. Do you want to hear about Liberia and Guinea and Sierra Leone and the Ivory Coast and the Congo and Zimbabwe and— soon—Nigeria?

Europe is not serious about Africa; it even neglects to service the consequences of its own earlier bargains, then made in the name of the colonial pact and ill-considered structural adjustments. Now the European Union recommends a neoliberal economy, which in practice means the perpetuation of authoritarian regimes, condemning Africa to further military turmoil and civil wars. Nation-states are becoming obsolete except as frameworks for sucking in foreign aid, and the field is left to drug-crazed "rebel" groups and religious "revolutionaries" associated with charismatic movements of an obscurantist nature. The logical outcome will be further decay of the social and political fabric, the continuing decline of conditions of life, the desperate attempts of people to get into Europe at all costs—and Fortress Europe's only response will be police repression.

How does one try and promote a culture of peace and a strategy of survival when countries are governed by belly politics, graft, corruption, and incompetence? How does one deal with the pandemics of AIDS and malaria when national medical systems have been dismantled in the name of financial soundness? What does one do about the crisis of education—the true reason for the upsurge of child soldiers and of Qur'anic schools—by now a major obstacle to the economic modernization of the continent, relegating the very ideas of "good governance" and the rule of law to the realms of fantasy? (It is not just me asking these questions; if you are interested in learning the facts, you may wish to consult *African Affairs* published by the Royal African Society in London.)

It is true in an absolute sense that we *know* no more than we knew before. In that there has been no progress. Every generation lives in the fullness of its own limited comprehension. Nor do we learn from the mistakes of the past—perhaps because we equate survival with progress, with the need to forge ahead. Maybe we are doomed to make the same errors. And it is true, as well, that we have to transcend our limitations, that we have to cling to the notion of a utopia as a justification and motivation for keeping on moving and making a noise. Our minds are as ever still bordered by darkness, but now we live in an infinitely more dangerous world.

And yet, I don't want to end on a desperate note. At the Gorée Institute, where I have been working for the last number of years, we try to understand and to learn the problems we face, to put into practice modules of metamorphosis and to observe the results and then to forge "tools" that can be used by others as well. We know that the shaping of perception, the search for understanding and interpreting the world we live in, can be considered an ancient and ongoing form of poetry. We know that it is possible to partake of the processes of expanding consciousness and of awareness making and thus—implicitly at least—promote a concern with larger responsibilities and with the ethics of evolving in such a harsh environment. Perhaps, too, we are motivated by a passion for the dialectic between the particular and the general, the subjective and the objective, and we therefore prize doubt, questioning, and the search for transformation. We are committed to remaining attentive to the enrichment of diversity. This underlies many of our concerns: the recognition and the valorization of diversity within the larger context of shared values (the utopia we cling to)—not as some expression of conservatism but as a precondition for sustainable survival; yes, for an approach to social and even political and economic *progress*; for renewal and growth in mutual respect, tolerance, and ultimately for decency and dignity. This implies according memory its rightful place and recognition, and promoting the comprehension between memory and imagination.

Progress? No. Creativity? Out of necessity. There may be no progress, but we have to keep on imagining ourselves. There may be no progress, but we must continue creating the premises of facts on the ground. The world—our world—has existed since all times, and every day we have to create it anew. If we did not walk the earth it would not exist.

Ek eet my brood en drink my wyn
en hou my hart van gode rein.
—N. P. Van Wyk Louw

(I eat my bread and drink my wine
and keep my heart free of gods.)

Seven

THE PITY AND THE HORROR

However much you feed a wolf, it always looks to the forest.
We are all wolves of the dense forest of Eternity.

—Marina Tsvetaeva

"You don't know me. There's no reason why you should and little cause for you to listen to what somebody like myself may have to say …"

That's what I wrote in an open letter to General Ariel Sharon on April 7, 2002. At the time he was the prime minister of Israel. A delegation of writers—Russell Banks, Juan Goytisolo, Bei Dao, José Saramago, Wole Soyinka, myself, and one or two more—had just returned from a short visit to the West Bank and to Gaza. We were guided by Elias Sanbar and Leila Chahid of the Palestinian Liberation Organization and accompanied by a film crew. We had gone there to see for ourselves, and to read in public together with Mahmoud Darwish and other Palestinian authors as a gesture of solidarity. After all, they were practically cut off from the outside world. Upon our return, each one of us tried to give an account of the experience. Mine took the form of this letter.

It continued: "Indeed, I don't imagine you have time to pay attention to views that do not correspond to your own. In fact, I'm convinced you do not listen to anybody who doesn't say what you wish to hear.

"Should it interest you, I'm a writer born in South Africa now living and working abroad. For some time back there I too grew up among a 'chosen people' who behaved as *Herrenvolk*—as all those who believe themselves singularized by suffering or entrusted with a special mission from God."

In the letter I apologized for the wound inflicted by the comparative allusion to the people of Israel as putative *Herrenvolk*, because of echoes from a recent past when, in Europe, so many Jews were the victims of a "final solution" imposed by a people who did describe themselves as a master race. But how else was one to illustrate the so-called "justification" for the comportment of Israel's army when one was flooded by the horror of their exactions?

These rough equivalences don't come lightly. As writer, I'm deeply apprised of the need to keep the words uncluttered of any urge to rouse easy emotions. This is what facile comparisons do—they nullify understanding the complexity of the observed phenomena by a rush of outrage heating the throat and staining the adversary with the vomit of borrowed or vicarious condemnation. Apartheid was not Nazism, though to say so was a striking slogan. And the policies perpetrated by Israeli forces on the Palestinian people should not be equated with Apartheid. Each one of these processes and systems was evil enough to merit a thorough description of its own historical singularity.

And yet ... there were similarities—and yes, differences: This blind competition, on both sides, to be recognized as more-victim-than-thou; cloaking atrocities in the "divine" right to self-defense; the shameless manipulation of perceptions and the mendacity; the concomitant brutalization of society; the disdain shown for the humanity of the Palestinians—indeed, denying even the most elementary humane treatment of a terrified and trapped civilian population ...

"It was all only too familiar. The underlying assumptions informing and "justifying" your actions are racist," I wrote to the general. "As was the case with the South African regime, the preferred methods by which you hope to subjugate the enemy consist of force and shedding blood and inflicting humiliation. Cynically, you think you can get away with this as long as you play up to what are described as the vital interests of the United States in the region. I don't think you really care a Haifa fig for American interests, do you?" (And why should he?)

He probably despised the Americans for being blinded by their own material crassness and their ignorance of the world, and he must have tired of having to keep on scrunching their balls, because of their own accord they were not going to last the course, being easily lured away by their narcissistic consumerism or by a partisan passion for other capers such as elections that they could steal. True, Sharon's used car salesman doppelgänger, Netanyahu, displayed his "craft" of crude propaganda and bold lies more openly there, and had considerable success with avid audiences, as if he were a dirty finger tweaking the clitoris of a swooning American public opinion. But you too, I wrote, by opportunistically echoing the semantically challenged American president (and putting words in his mouth) who describes every "other" as a terrorist, have shown that you take the rest of the world for fools. Surely, not all of us agree that the highest good in the world is America's greed for cheap oil, and that we should therefore be expected to adhere to the inviolability of corrupt regimes in the region!

A more pernicious red herring needs to be smelled out. It is blatantly averred, again and again, that any criticism of Israel's policies is an expression of anti-Semitism. With that assertion the argument is supposed to be closed and sealed. (A softer version of the above position, with the same aim, would be that one should refrain from criticizing Israel as this will play into the hands of overt or closet anti-Semites, because the belly of the beast is still fertile and one does not know how poisonously loaded certain references and words still echo.) Of course, I reject this attempt at censorship and intellectual bullying that intends to disqualify the grounds for debate. No amount of suffering—be it of the Tutsis, the Kurds, the Armenians, the Vietnamese, the Bosnians, or the Palestinians—can confer immunity from critical assessment. (And, to put it sadly, no amount of suffering would seem to inoculate people against visiting the same vile practices they were subjected to upon others.) Draping oneself in the cloak of elected holiness and a self-proclaimed exceptional status, or hiding behind the purported promise of some Holy Land promulgated by One God of Jealousy and Intolerance, cannot excuse the crimes carried out by an invading and occupying army. For that matter, the mirror actions of massacring innocents in cold blood, as ordered by fanatic warlords in the name of Resistance, is as unacceptable. No reference to some ostensibly sacrosanct "Greater Israel" can camouflage the fact that the settlements are armed colonies built on land shamelessly stolen from the Palestinians, festering there as shards in their flesh, or operating as snipers' nests intended to thwart and annul any possibility of Palestinian statehood. There can be no way to peace through the annihilation of the other, even when he's an Arab, just as there can be no paradise for the "martyr."

This "anti-Semitism" allegation is utterly deplorable, especially coming from Jewish intellectuals who so often constitute the reasonable, rational, humanist, and creative backbone of Western societies.

Why should we be subjected to this special pleading or look the other way when it is Israel committing the unconscionable? Is what's sauce for the goose then, in some Yahweh-inspired way, not sauce for the kosher gander?

"No, General Sharon" (I wrote): "past injustices suffered cannot justify or gloss over your present fascist actions. A viable state cannot be built on the expulsion of another people who have as much claim to that territory as you have. Might is not right. In the long run your immoral and shortsighted policies will furthermore undermine Israel's legitimacy as a state."

I explained to the general how my letter had grown from the opportunity of visiting the territories for the first time. (And yes, I'm afraid they can reasonably be described as resembling Bantustans, for only too often are they reminiscent of the ghettos and the controlled camps of misery one knew in South Africa.) I only glimpsed Israel briefly, upon entering and then later leaving after spending a night in the opulent but dismally deserted David Intercontinental Hotel of Tel Aviv—and after being quizzed by a young female immigration official whether I had slept with any Palestinian woman! You may say my impressions are fatally one-sided. Perhaps. Certainly, I didn't see much of Israel, though one is never out of sight of Israeli demarcation lines, checkpoints, tanks, and armed outposts in the West Bank.

I wondered, General Sharon: are your two nations really all that different? You are of a similarly diverse mixture of cultures and origins, you are all of you diaspora people, and you are equally intelligent and quick-witted and excitable. You may well be brave in a similar fashion. On both sides there are creative minds of exceptional integrity at work. On both sides, also, there are an extraordinary number of self-serving, power-hungry, obtuse individuals, fanatics with their spirits obfuscated by this God-nonsense—or using it as a pretext.

As provocateur—cold-blooded and cruel—you, Ariel Sharon, stand out among your peers. In your dogged but ill-considered attempts to subvert previous agreements and to scupper the possibility of peace—except for the peace of the graveyard and of scattering premised on the "total transfer" or "disappearance" of the Palestinian entity—you are bringing turmoil to the region. This you probably planned, like some Samson pulling down the pillars of the edifice on foe and friend alike. It remains to be seen whether the inaudible growling of your principals in Washington will inflect your campaign of calculated terror and wanton destruction—or whether it is but a slap on the wrist, a smokescreen behind which to better align the "free world's" war on "terror," and (in passing) for the domination of resources and a global control of markets and water and cheap oil and, insultingly, for imposing "democracy."

The few days I'd spent in Palestine with the World Parliament of Writers delegation left me with a mixed bag of strong but conflicting impressions. How small the country is! How inextricably linked the two peoples are! The stones, the stones everywhere. The topography of names familiar from the Bible. The beautiful light. The attempts to make the place look like some Switzerland by planting out-of-place conifers. The inhospitality of the land, except for lush coastal plains. How abysmally sad the villages, reminding one of the lifeless and apathetic towns of East Germany. The green lights in the mosques and all the unfinished habitations. The ugliness of the architecture everywhere, the ubiquitous light-gray limestone building blocks. The inanity of the invasion and the occupation—all those lit-up detour roads built for the exclusive use of settlers and Israeli citizens. The surly pettiness of the controls at checkpoints—having little to do with security and everything to do with the primitive urge to humiliate, frustrate, harass, and drive to insane rage a confined population. The extreme youth of the occupant soldiers, and sadly, that they are so obviously well-cultivated boys and girls. The ruthless rapaciousness with which Israel destroys the possible Palestinian economy and steals their money and their goods. The ancient revenge: bulldozing houses, uprooting olive groves (I believe one can buy beautiful old trees for a song in Israel). The equally primitive sight of armed positions under camouflage netting and Israeli flags in commandeered houses. The defilement of Palestinian public places. The vaunted "democratic" Israeli media knowingly lying to their own people, denying the war crimes carried out by their troops, haggling like souk merchants about the exact number of houses flattened "accidentally." The Berlin walls around the settlements in Gaza (and behind them university extensions, research institutes, American-linked hotels, golf courses: all the illusions of "normal" opulence), and then the rubble of destroyed Palestinian quarters looking now like Ground Zero. The way little "refugee camp" kids looked us straight in the eye, apparently uncowed, but then we were told they're probably all traumatized not only by the hovering dogs of your gun ships, General Sharon, and your antediluvian tanks and your men in battle gear shooting at everything that moves, but as well by all the hyperactive adults surrounding them. The old kerchiefed women in the narrow alley of some recently attacked camp screaming that you, Sharon, will never make them depart and that they chased away your soldiers "like dogs." Screaming abuse, also, at the spineless Arab states and the cowardice of their own Palestinian Authority.

The ebullience of the intellectuals and artists under siege in Ramallah—arguing, laughing at their own plight. How they all say:

"We don't want to be heroes, we don't want to be victims, we just want to lead normal lives." Their wry despair. Mahmoud Darwish: "There is too much history and too many prophets in this small land." The visit to Abu Amar, Yasser Arafat, a holed fox, his trembling wax-yellow hands clinging to the empty clichés of "a peace of the brave" and "the conscience of the international community." A bourgeois lady lamenting the desecration of the Palestinian landscape. And a human rights lawyer claiming: "We are grateful to Sharon for two things—he united all the Palestinian factions and he took away every option except to resist." (Famous last, wishful words!) Later on the same haunted man, chain-smoking and with the sweat of death already on him, remarked bitterly that repression had now penetrated the skin of the people and therefore they had nothing except their skins with which to defend themselves. Hence the human bombs.

For these, I wrote to the general, will be my contrasted conclusions: You have not broken the spirit of the Palestinian people. Quite the contrary—they are now more resolute than ever to build a state; it doesn't matter how much you bully them. They saw the renewed onslaught coming, they knew you were but playing footsy with General Zinni, probably primed to do so by Dick Cheney. They also know that since you have now made them stronger you must strike harder and deeper because you are caught in a conundrum of your own making. Like Bush in his crusade against the infidel and the disobedient you have to accelerate your distension of international public ethics and flaunt common sense even more, and throw good moral money after bad political calculations. They know that nothing they can do will appease you short of turning turtle. (Or committing suicide quietly, far away from Israeli agglomerations.) They fear you will have to compound this crime against humanity, which you are committing at present, that you may indeed break their hopes for a secular, modern, democratic, and viable state accountable to its population, and bring forth the devil among them. They also know this will profoundly divide and weaken Israel.

But you don't care, do you?

This is the pity and the horror.

◆

Time passed. The letter I'd written to Sharon earned me a load of criticism, as was to be expected (did I really expect otherwise?)— vituperation, and even abuse. Claude Lanzman, the respected French filmmaker of *Shoa*, published a two-sheet essay in *Le Monde* aimed against Wole Soyinka, Juan Goytisolo, and myself (José Saramago was beyond even naming since he had compared conditions in the West Bank to Auschwitz), illustrating why I in particular (such a promising poet in my time) had become a virulent anti-Semite. Fritz Raddatz wrote an open letter to the *Frankfurter Allgemeine Zeitung* under the title: "Sie sind infam, mein Freund" etc.

But then I remembered the text written and read by Mahmoud Darwish on the day we visited the Sakakini Cultural Centre in Ramallah. (A few days later Israeli soldiers retaliating against a particularly lethal suicide bomb attack in Israel were to sack the centre; everything would be ripped apart and the Star of David splotched on the walls.) "What is the place of poetry in these barbaric times?" Darwish had asked in a soft voice, peering myopically through thick glasses ...

> Poetry is fragile despite its metaphorical recourse to the power of silk and the firmness of honey. Fragile, because its work to change the soul and make the heart bigger is slow and invisible. And so, even though it

unites the intimate with the universal, it cannot escape its image as daughter of solitude and of the outer edge, like an echo rising from an obscure dream ... The poets should not deny that solitude, nor glorify it, but must continue being the eternal travelers between their interior and the outside. It's up to them to lighten the load of questions about the usefulness of poetry.

It is they who ought to renew the anxiety of their art by even more creative anxiety because they will never find an immune theory against the poetic irruption ...

Mankind is now in a "state of emergency."

◆

Then, on August 10, 2008, I heard the terrible news that Mahmoud Darwish had passed away.

Much had happened in the intervening years. General Sharon had decided, unilaterally, to withdraw Israeli troops from the Gaza Strip and dismantle some settlements there. It became evident that this was, unfortunately, not to be the beginning of a comprehensive peace agreement that would finally allow for the coming about of a viable Palestinian state on contingent territory, but part of a strategy to consolidate Palestine's dismantlement and to tighten the noose around the West Bank so as to further destroy their hopes for survival as a distinct people. A Wall of Shame was constructed, annexing even more Palestinian land and cutting villages off from their fields. Israel has an ancestral knowledge of ghettos.

And Ariel Sharon was felled by a massive stroke. What a strange fate! He'd probably been his happiest as a farmer in the desert, making the barrenness bloom and maybe looking for lost sheep. Something about the personage spoke to me from my own past; I'd known farmer warriors just like him—tough, gruff, and cunning, and often at odds with their own hierarchies and with the soft-palmed city dwellers. Bar-rel-chested people who killed easily and abundantly, even though they often held deep religious convictions. People who, finally and stoically, despaired of history and of human nature.

Did he even know about my "open letter"? Had I been unfair to single him out? Did I give in to the easy demagoguery of outrage in a place where I would not have to pay any price and where I was not equipped to recognize the irrationality of pain?

Sharon did not die. In fact, as I write this now in 2008, he is still alive somewhere, in a coma. Rather, kept "alive" like some vegetable or a crystal being cared for by the best that medical science can muster—with no possible future and nowhere to come back to. Where? A crypt? In a sterilized room? In a desert cave, perhaps?

There followed the ill-fated war by Israel against Lebanon, the invasion of the southern part and the attempts to wreak as much de-struction as possible on that country's infrastructure, with blind but methodical malevolence. There followed, in Gaza—as was inevitable, given the humiliation of sham "negotiations" without any tangible re-sults ever, and of relentless pressure and of targeted assassinations and of destroying the credibility of the PLO, and precipitated by the cor-ruption of the cadres—the implosion of Palestinian unity and coher-ence, with faction turning against faction in street battles. A people were now to be beggared and starved, their dream destroyed.

I had met Mahmoud Darwish again. I was privileged to participate in an homage to him in Aix-en-Provence. He had been dangerously ill in the meantime, some heart disease ran in the veins of his family, he had undergone an operation with his chest cut open, spent time in a coma. From this dark visit to the underground emerged an enigmatic but brave volume of poems, *Mural*. His friends gathered around; we sat on terraces under plane trees of that southern town of troubadours and Pétanque players. We smoked cigars and drank wine. For a while there was light and there were birds and Mahmoud made teasing remarks. Arab-speaking immigrant workers had come from afar, from all over the region to pack the auditorium where he read his poetry. It always happened. It reminded me of that night we read with him on the stage of a theater in Ramallah—how absolutely full and rapt the place was with poor people who'd walked over the hills in darkness, avoiding Israeli checkpoints, to now stand for hours shoulder to shoulder, how they collectively breathed back at him lines of his verses, and how he joked that they should elect the donkey as a national symbol. There are times when the moon actually smells of wonderfully odorous crushed herbs and of stones.

◆

The news of his death brought anguish and a pain that were nearly unbearable.

Again, some of us had the luck, only a few weeks earlier, of listening to him reading his lines in an arena in Arles. The sun was setting, there was a soundless wind in the trees and from the neighboring streets we could hear the voices of children playing. And for hours we sat on the ancient stone seats, spellbound by the depth and the beauty of this poetry. Was it about Palestine? Was it about his people dying, the darkening sky, the intimate relationships with those on the other side of the wall, "soldier" and "guest," exile and love, the return to what is no longer there, the memory of orchards, the dreams of freedom …?

Yes—like a deep stream all of these themes were there, of course, since they so constantly informed his verses; but it was also about olives and figs and a horse against the skyline and the feel of cloth and the mystery of the color of a flower and the eyes of a beloved and the imagination of a child and the hands of a grandfather. And of death. Gently, repeatedly, terribly, by implication, mockingly, even longingly—death.

Many of us were petrified. Maybe we sensed—I remember seeing Leila Chahid's downcast eyes and trembling lips—that this was like saying goodbye. Like this? On foreign soil? Time stopped there, and the lament was made nearly joyous in the ageless rhythm of the two Palestinian brothers in black on their string instruments accompanying the words coming to us from the earth and from a light blowing over that distant land. We wanted to weep, and yet there was laughter and he made it easy for us and it became festive.

Afterwards, I remember, we did not want to leave the place. Light had fallen but we lingered, embracing and holding one another. Strangers looked each other in the eye, fumbled for a few words to exchange, some thoughts. How awkward it has become to be moved! I remember thinking how deeply he touched us, how generous he was. And how light. Maybe, had he known, he would have wanted to take leave in this way. No drama. No histrionics. No demagogic declarations. Maybe not even much certainty anymore. Despair, yes—and laughter. The dignity and the humbleness of the combatant. And somehow, without us knowing or understanding, his wanting to comfort us. He said he was stripping his verses of everything but the poetry. He was reaching out even more profoundly than he'd ever done before for the universally shared fate and sense of being human. Perhaps he was trying to convey that it was now time to "remember to die."

The next day when we left, when we said goodbye in that Hotel Nord-Pinus with its huge posters of corridas and the photos of bullfighters fragile like angels in the intimacy of preparing for walking out into the blinding light, with the sweet smell of death lilies in the foyer, I wanted to kiss his hands and he refused.

Time will pass. There will be eulogies and celebrations. He will be "official," a "voice of the people" … He knew all of that and he accepted it, and sometimes he gently mocked the hyperbole and the impossible expectations. Maybe the anger will be forgotten. Maybe even, the politicians will refrain from trying to steal the light of his complex legacy, his questioning and his doubts, and perhaps some cynics—abroad as well—would, this time, not disgust us with the spectacle of their crocodile tears.

Mahmoud is gone. The exile is over. He will not have lived to see the end of the suffering of his people—the mothers and the sons and the children who cannot know why they should be born into the horror of this life, the arbitrary cruelty of their dying. He will not fade away. Not the silhouette in its dapper outdated clothes and polished loafers, not the intelligent eyes behind the thick lenses, not the teasing, not the curiosity about the world and the intimacy of his reaching out to those close to him, not the sharp analyses of the foibles and the folly of politics, not the humanism, not the good drinking and the many cigarettes, not the hospitality of never imposing his pain on you, not the voice that spoke from the ageless spaces of poetry, not the verses, not the verses, not the timeless love-making of his words.

◆

In writing this, looking back over the few glimpses I could get of the horror and the pity, I just wanted to reach out to you. And as I write another ghost image arises from the words on the page: the face of Yehuda Amichai, the Israeli poet—a friend of mine and a friend of

Mahmoud's. I remember a poem he'd written—of an Israeli father looking for his lost son and a Palestinian shepherd looking for a lamb gone astray, both of them walking over the bare yellow hills of the Valley of Death, and how their calls echo and meet.

I told Mahmoud in Arles how I want to propose to my fellow poets that we should, each one of us, declare ourselves "honorary Palestinians." He tried to laugh it away with the habitual embarrassment of a brother. Perhaps, without meaning to, I was blundering into areas of shyness and of a sadness that had stained the folds of the land too deeply to be talked about. Was he not also thinking of the voices in Amichai's poem? And indeed, our attempts to approach and understand the inconsolable can only be puny and clumsy. We cannot die or write in the place of his people, in the place of Mahmoud Darwish. Yet, somehow, however futile the gesture, I needed to try and say that the gift of his poetry is of importance to all of us in the world, that it grows from a particular light and soil, certainly, carrying the articulations of a very specific struggle and a life that had become word, but that it is also reaching out to our universal consciousness and condition. And that it would be an honor to try and understand ourselves through an understanding of where his poetry came from.

It was already too late. He was leaving. He is gone. But by sharing these fleeting moments with you, I'm sure, we are celebrating the dignity and the beauty of his life.

Some of you, I know, probably cried as I did then and am doing now, when you heard of the death of the poet so far away from home, in Houston of all places. And most of you never even met him!

Maybe, as we cry out for what is lost, we will pause somewhere because we hear a flutter of birds overhead, and hold a protecting hand to our blinded eyes as we search the sky for that darkened rhythm.

Eight

THE NOMADIC CONVERSATION

with Mahmoud Darwish

when you die, Mahmoud
when your aorta thrashing
like a purple snake bursts
because the lines can no longer
carry the perfect metaphor
and your heart as poem spurts
the final blood
in that hospital in foreign parts
of the barbarian land,
when your heart at last
could be a wingless bird

a moon starts growing above the island
among slithering clouds
of this 'little winter season'
which soon will spill dark ink
in long verses over the waves
so that crows and goats and dirt-poor children
in song may plash in the mud
as if celebrating liberation

three, four, five days and nights
invisible by day, invisible like dying
or the movement surfacing in a stanza words,

decay in the night
when time takes its time as reaper
over the fields of the body

until the loose fleece fades
and shadows over the naked land
fall away like tufts of flesh
and the moon bloats virginally full

a sloop of bone
your skull, Mahmoud

◆

cover me quickly, you said
no wailing and no grand display
write at best a blinding quatrain
so that the object of your poem's pain
may be eclipsed
there's no identity
just a soughing space of shiver
all is movement until it stops moving
to sing,
time is the timeless lover
over image patterns of the skin

drape no flag over my coffin, you said
a flag is to have a shirt cut from its cloth
for the homeless
a flag is the rag with which the clown
teaches a child in the circus of color
and the blur of betrayal
our flag blows free to remember the Nakba

when olive trees were wrapped in dead fire
while bird coops of verse were written for us

just this, just this

let there be music, you said
a feast with much laughter for my friends
and a glass of wine lifted high to the day
as red as the ringing throb and wash of a heart

Nine

HOW WE KILL, KILL, KILL

LETTER TO MY AMERICAN FRIEND
Dakar, March 8, 2003

Joe, please receive these random thoughts at countdown time.

It is the eighth of March. In a few days, it now seems certain and ineluctable, thousands of people will die stupidly and violently.

Nothing new. The human species is dumb though sly, and violent though tender. But this time round the killing spree has been more cynically prepared and more nakedly for greed and power lust, the ritual celebration of distant death brought about by sophisticated weapons systems more rigorously foretold, the lies in the teeth less elaborate—maybe because the principal actors are more mundane and their tongues more wooden. Now grown primates with marking on their faces will make real the boys' games of snuffing out life in a bloody sandpit. The banality of evil, of killing "to save lives."

The USA is engaged in waging war on the world. You must know it. As during the Cold War, the language is once again confiscated and public discourse perverted to a reduced number of emphatically repeated phrases ringing with emptiness so as to justify the aggression. The words we will hear most often now, in a froth of semireligious self-righteousness, will be "evil" and "terrorism." I haven't heard the say-all, mean-nothing label of "terrorism" bandied about with such abandon since the South Africa of the '70s and the '80s when even I was declared a statutory "terrorist." It makes me feel quite giddy with nostalgia for the good old days! There will be a turning inside out of the concepts of "freedom" and "peace." After all, President Bush is saying in as many words that America has to wage war preemptively in order to ensure peace; or that, so as to impose respect for international law, America has to topple sovereign foreign governments.

And to flesh out the argument, here is Ms. Condoleezza Rice stating: "Preemption is anticipatory self-defense," that is, the right of the United States to attack any country that it *thinks* could attack it first. Reaction will precede action. But be careful, she warns! Other nations "should not use preemption as a pretext for aggression."

What does this mean? I see where Bruce Cumings from the University of Chicago analyzes it as follows: "Now we will have pre-emptive attacks, "counterproliferation" (*what a barbaric word!*) for everyone except ourselves and our allies, untold billions for the Pentagon to dissuade any and all comers from "a military build-up in hopes of surpassing, or equaling, the power of the United States," and endless wars into the disappearing and newly darkening future to "rid the world of evil."

There are method and continuity in the hubris. In the run-up to this crazy narrative of an "announced" war I came across a reference to the Republican James Burnham, cofounder of the *National Review*, who already thought that "the unparalleled supremacy" of the American military would continue into the indefinite future, who denounced internationalism as appeasement and error, and containment as too passive, and who argued for a "World Empire" based on America's superiority in atomic weapons—shall we say "weapons of mass destruction"?—while querying why the bomb could not be wielded to "make politically possible the domination of the world by a single sufficiently large state." This was 1947. Burnham had then urged Washington to "join the offensive to liberate Russia," rather in similar terms that Bush wants to liberate Iraq and Sharon Palestine. Ultimately, surely, as it was then already: so that the rich might become richer and liberated from the fear of poverty.

◆

I write these lines at the Charles de Gaulle Airport in Paris while waiting for my flight to Dakar. The terminals are unusually and eerily quiet. The embarkation too will be quite different from the normal jostling rush to get on board; only a passel of "undesirables" will nonchalantly keep up their bedraggled appearance as they are escorted on to the plane for the trip back to square one. Many seats will be empty. It is as if people are waiting, resigned or fearful or stunned, for this thing of man-made horror to be unleashed finally. Enough waiting already!

It's been a balmy, sunny day in old Europe, as if tinged by a premature spring in the air. With heart in throat and a stone in the stomach one remembers that only yesterday, and still today, life was "normal": children going to school, young people kicking a ball around a vacant lot, lovers exchanging sweet messages on their cellular telephones, *madames* walking their poodles and madams their dogs ... It is good to be alive, isn't it?

So why die? Why inflict death?

On board I watch the news: a young GI with painted cheeks talks about the "adventure" of going abroad for the first time (maybe the last also); a white-clad human bomb in Baghdad says he has no fear of dying a "martyr." Don't they know that the only experience worth having— the only one we *know*—is life?

These adolescent wolves are weirdly innocent. The real killers, the ideologues and the fanatics, maybe too corrupt and twisted to still experience the shiver of ejaculation, are elsewhere in their war rooms with the maps of "scientific" knowledge and control on the walls. How puny the targets seem. How abstract and dreamlike. Should one be surprised, distraught perhaps, by this surge of macho bestiality? Is it unusual that again even some intellectuals will exult in the bloody tough-mindedness of being "realistic," showing their "naturalness" by dirtying their hearts, giving proof of the kick they too may experience at not being lily-livered ivory tower dwellers?

I don't want to think about it. I don't want to pretend to some geopolitical understanding of the murderous folly. For now, in this lull between destinations, I want to be maudlin and remember our shared humanity.

We're going to be subjected to strong emotions and much brutalization, exposed to the lures of desperate simplifications. I hope we won't be driven apart and that, come shock and awe and hell or high water, we will continue to honor our joint memories of dreaming about the possible dignity of human existence.

Yet, we have to think some things through. How do we get out of the box of defending, even if only by default, the actions and the attitudes of despicable dictators who will now be presented as sacrificial sheep? When you have crazed warmongers running your government in Washington, what feasible resilience can democracy still have? How can we—you and us—effectively help oppose and undo the imposition of American imperial world power? Must we go underground then, revert to clandestine resistance, to the rotting romanticism of whispered codes and invisible ink? Surely, only you from within the fertile belly of the ravenous beast can effectively weaken the monster. How do we live with the shame of being predators? How do we realize the victory for humanity that will be putting Saddam and his generals together with Bush and his acolytes in the international dock, accused of crimes against humanity? And how can we help conceive of a *beyond*, of an international arrangement of a new kind (please, let's not think of it as a New World Order)? How do we stop committing suicide? How do we foster some respect for life, maybe even for decency?

It is dark outside now. We too are flying over an ancient map: first over Lorca's chanted Córdoba of the dark horses; then Casablanca where Bogey lisped; Meknes, Safi, Essaouira where descendants of black slaves dance their mystical raptures; Ouarzazate off to the left; Agadir; Nouakchott; dark moon and dark desert, and soon we'll descend toward Dakar Yoff. I'm told the Harmattan has been breathing its gray breath of late over leaf and windowsill. Most of my fellow Africans in the half-empty aircraft are dozing. I watched them peruse the papers. What are they thinking? Perhaps this coming war will be experienced in Africa with wry relief that other, more sophisticated barbarians elsewhere, are also stupidly dying in large numbers. But of course, for all of us it will be another defeat in the struggle for democracy, a further invalidation of the modernist project.

Forgive me my naive mumbling. It may come across as the murmuring of some gladiator saluting his brothers as he slopes off to die. And of course it is not that. You won't catch me on any front. Like you, I hope, I too will be sitting on the outskirts watching from the bleachers and puking in my paper bag. Nevertheless, this is *our war*. I (and

I'm sure many of you too) go into this with despair, with disgust, with death in the soul. Those who dreamed, planned, plotted the atrocities and will now be ordering the mass dying are people like us. Yes, even Rumsfeld and Cheney and Saddam Hussein—so very similar in their delirium of destruction—are ordinary humans. And those who will die are people like us; they're our people, except that most of them are innocent. They will die in terror. They will also die for nothing. Indeed, man is a wolf to man. And a mad dog.

◆

It could well be that one war camouflages another, that putting America in an orange alert state of continuous war and occupation (already the bases are mushrooming all over the world, including Africa, and soon proconsuls will be named), retching and ratcheting up the prostitute notion of patriotism, will permit the moral rearmament forces of darkness to sweep clean the home stage of all your raucous minorities, your uncouth thinkers, and your uncloseted deviants.

For again, as it was during the Cold War, one senses that the general climate inside your country is one of intimidation and, concomitantly, that it will bring about a distension of the limits of the acceptable, both in ethical and legal terms. A coalition of Muslims, Arabs, and South Asians already points out that since September 11, 2001, thousands of them, now racially and religiously pegged, have been detained and held incommunicado because they ostensibly "fit the profile of a threat to national security," but that not one person has been charged with a crime related to the attack on the World Trade Center or the Pentagon or any other terrorism-related event; that many of them are held as "material witnesses" or "enemy combatants," with no access to family, friends, or lawyers, and that the government has said it intends to hold these men without trials until the war ends—which, according to Vice President Cheney, may last several generations; that they have been stripped of due process rights such as innocence until proven guilty, the right to legal representation and to lawyer-client privilege, the right to defend themselves in an open trial; that since November 2001 any non-U.S. citizen can thus be tried by military tribunal for being a terrorist, aiding or harboring a terrorist, that such a person may be sentenced to death in secret with evidence withheld from him or her and his or her lawyer, and such a condemned "invisible one" will not be allowed to appeal the sentence to either a U.S. state or federal or international court; that in November 2001, the Department of Justice ordered five thousand men who had entered the country legally over the past few years—all of them Muslim, Arab, or South Asian—to submit to "voluntary" interrogations and that in March 2002 another three thousand men were added to the list; that many immigration hearings of the detainees are held in secret and that John Ashcroft's Justice Department has the right to keep in custody any non-citizen even if an immigration judge has ordered him or her freed; that domestic spying on international students includes information on what classes they take, what grades they get, what jobs they have, what extracurricular activities they indulge in—all this under the constant threat of deportation or detention for things like protesting or even taking less than a full-time credit load, and that FBI agents now have the authority to observe private gatherings without first obtaining a warrant. Already now, as a foreigner needing a visa for the United States, I found that one signs away one's right to question and oppose arbitrary arrest and deportation.

◆

Don't you think this American aggression and the attacks upon the world are informed by structural economic and social injustices at home? On board I leaf through a study made by Paul Krugman and published in the *New York Times Magazine*, showing that the thirteen thousand richest families in America now have almost as much income as the twenty million poorest. And those thirteen thousand families have incomes three hundred times that of average families! Krugman points out that the average American salary rose by about 10 percent over the last thirty years—from $32,522 in 1970 to $35,864 in 1999. "Over the same period, however, the average real annual compensation of the top one hundred CEO's went from $1.3 million—thirty-nine times the pay of an average worker—to $37.5 million, more than one thousand times the pay of ordinary workers."

We're talking of a 2,500 percent rise in CEO incomes!

◆

There again, we must start thinking of *afterward*. What comes after Bush and his gauleiters who, surely, must be as unrepresentative of the majority of ordinary decent folk in America as Saddam Hussein and his mustached clones are of the 100 percent who "voted" for him?

A fiery actuality will burn itself out, become ashes and salt on the paper. By the time I can get my letter to you published (if ever), this particular war might be done. (Then again, it might not.) The actors who now loom so large will have become shades. Soon it will mean nothing. Who will remember the squint-eyed "dry drunk" president? Who will be able to recall the names of his entourage—the fundamentalist vice president with the flabby body full of Machiavellian lies and a bitter vengefulness, the reincarnated SS general as defense secretary

a walking validation of Mengele's dream, the Christian fanatic justice
minister with the small feet who felt his soul surging and mating with
God at every execution, the racist desk-hawks, the closet fascists, the
"house nigger" secretary of state (as opposed to the yard slave, according
to Harry Belafonte's definition), the arid black lady whose only ecstasy
would seem to have been the privilege of pleasing the boss? Maybe,
by the time this is read, their names will be smeared in blood over the
pages of history.

◆

How will we come out of it? And will we have asked the right questions? Why generalize? I don't believe in the concept of "evil." It
smacks of predestination. Are there national characteristics though?
Could there be an innate, nearly genetic historical memory? Maybe
we could point at traces of what may be called cultural memes. But
surely, despite our animal instincts, people must be *conditioned* to
be violent. Surely, the ceaseless fostering of the *right* to gratification
and to profit, the cultivation of narcissism and a competitive egotism,
the blind fear of falling down the slippery slopes of a society that has
no safety nets, the arrogance of a belief in God and in the superior
manifest destiny of imposing its will on the world must account for
the cruelty of American life, for the cultivation of desire and greed
and illusions, for the acceptance of incorporated quotidian lies in all
conceivable fields. How else do we explain the seemingly generalized
condoning of doing death, as in capital punishment—as if it were
"normal" and "democratic"?

How will we come out of it? Probably humbled and confused. But
that's still a long way off because all signs are that this war is intended

to be total and without end and will affect and maybe end the lives of people far away from the actual battlefields. I have no truck with the god of the Arabs or the Jews or the Christians—that fount head of cruelty. A pox on all their monotheist houses! But I nearly wish I did accept such an Existence so that I might pray: "Please God, be kind to the Palestinians in this tempest of their scattering. Save them from annihilation. And stop the Israelis from losing their souls."

Abraham Lincoln is reputed to have said: "I don't know what the soul is, / but whatever it is, I know it can humble itself."

◆

I thought I'd reach out before death comes raining down. I cannot wish you a good war, but I do hope you succeed in *passer entre les gouttes,* in avoiding the drops. May the ink of anger and sorrow somehow convey a memory of the blood of the innocents.

Let's stay in contact. Let's survive.

Ten

YOU SCREWS!

In a long life of strange encounters—discussing land rights with Aborigines in Sydney, their eyes so dark they must glow in the night, talking revolution with Tuaregs perched on their camels on a sand dune outside Timbuktu, the heads swathed in indigo cloth, exchanging philosophical thoughts with an aged courtesan in a Saigon bar, her thighs flabby but still softly white, or visiting the shivering silence-layers of millions of Monarch butterflies clustering to tall pines on the high mountain peaks of Michoacan, a smokeless pyre of prayers—this, for me, must rate as one of the most unexpected. I never thought the day would come when I, an ex-convict (a *bandiet* as we say in South Africa), would be asked to address an international gathering of screws in peaceful and antiseptic surroundings like here in Leeuwaarden in the Dutch "countryside"!

It is a tall order. After all, you collectively must know far more about the subject, I'd even say the *condition*, than I or any other prisoner ever could. This is why you are here in congress, coming as you do from your institutions in Cambodia and Tajikistan and Peru and Italy and all the other barely visible outcrops of what I'd call the Middle World—to exchange experiences and refine methods. I heard you speak of inmates as *economic units* and your honorable compounds as *enterprises*; I observed how at night you got drunk on cigars and gin and thigh-slapping prison stories, and I tried to be as unnoticed as possible in your comradely company. What could I, the only reprobate Christian among a pride of lions, tell you? Wouldn't it be utterly preposterous for me to want to teach grandmothers how to suck eggs or old dogs new tricks?

Do I even *want* to talk about prison? Can I still do so? Years ago, I went to listen to Jorge Luis Borges, the ancient mariner as blind Argentinean author giving a talk in Paris. Afterwards, somebody in the audience asked him whether he had committed suicide recently. No, he answered, he had given it up for quite some time already. "I've lost my hand." Similarly, I can claim I haven't been "inside" for a while now and I normally resent all attempts at dragging me back, particularly when coming from the sentimentally deprived (and depraved) or the vicarious heart-eaters and self-shitters who wallow in victimization and heroism by proxy. I can affirm that it is already a life ago since I last died.

(The story is told about how Borges, director of the National Library in Buenos Aires, his eyes watery and white with darkness, would leave his office every night and then wait patiently on the sidewalk of a busy thoroughfare for some Samaritan to guide him across to the literary café on the other side where he'd meet his cronies. And one night as he waited again a hand grabbed hold of his elbow and they started crossing the street with its blaring vehicles. As they arrived on the other side the anonymous person let go of Borges' arm and said, "Thank you, kind sir, for helping me across; not many people are that considerate to a poor blind man anymore.")

Borges was a great visitor of labyrinths. In my own prison writings I too have repeatedly used the metaphor of the Minotaur, the strange dark beast living in the empty heart of the maze whose head you must cut off and bring out if you want to continue living and, perhaps, save the city. Or even just to save face, because to the prisoner pushing or doing his time the Minotaur is ultimately himself, the Mirror. And the prisoner searches for his face the way a monster dreads the looking glass.

The myth echoes with ironies. When Theseus, who went into the Place (the Sanctuary) to kill the Minotaur, emerges with the severed head dripping blood, he forgets to give the correct signal of victory and the king his father jumps into the sea in despair. Does this imply that one's "inside" knowledge is of no consequence to the "outside" world? That one cannot convey experience? That there is no way of being intimate with strangers?

Of course, I only need to close my eyes to be back inside with the same overpowering sense of apathy and resignation, of having no power or say over my own destiny or even destination, and the same urgent and concrete need to start making the right connections for survival: how to get hold of some extra sugar, forbidden reading matter, a decent pair of pants that will actually fit, string for sending messages down the corridor ... Already I'm slipping back into that parallel world as familiar as an underground. It was to be living in the mirror as in a sea, secret and senseless and selfish like the shellfish. Everything that exists outside you can find inside as well, though perhaps distorted, bloated, or flattened. My nostrils would pick up the smell of the many nuances of grayness, of living rot; my ears become more alert because my view will be restricted. The clanging reverberations of steel doors and bare corridors replace the murmur of a carpeted world. I am stripped of the comfort of a known aesthetic hierarchy: the shadows on the wall have the same value and beauty as a Rembrandt painting. I shall also slip back into our own vernacular. If you ask somebody how he's doing, he will say, "I survive"; the word for friend is "connection"; thinking is described as "eating head"; the outside world is referred to as "the States," an unattainable mirage. One prison I was in—Poestoria Maximum Security where people used to be executed, given one lesson only in the art of flying with no wings and with ropes around their necks—was known to us, wryly, as Beverley Hills; the Diepkloof prison of Johannesburg ("Diepkloof" means Deep Gulch), now as desperately overcrowded as ever, is still called Sun City by the inmates. Maybe these fancy names are in reaction to the warders always saying: "Don't think this is a five-star hotel!"

At night there will be the murmur and the sighs of shellfish devouring one another, the slow crackle of skin being torn; with daylight maybe the severed head of an unlucky sacrifice will be found perched on the windowsill of a crowded cell, its disembodied smile obsequious to the masters for when you have devoured the flesh of the beast you are left with a grin of teeth, and nobody will know who the killers were but people will have crusts of dried blood around the lips. I am told the "punishment" of a recalcitrant gang member or the induction of a fresh arrival is now to be gang-raped and thus infected with HIV. Why should the innocent be allowed to live? What else can we pass on to one another except the knowledge of death?

All contact with my fellow humans will be reduced to the basic expressions and tricks of desire and fear. I once more start inventing a past and imagining a future so as to circumvent the present or imbue it with some sense of purpose. Purpose is always invented. The human animal is alive again—sentimental, superstitious, sly.

◆

This, the above, I thought I'd left behind; that the slate had been wiped clean and the state evacuated; no more lingering decayed shellfish smells. But the memories keep on returning. On streets or in trains I instinctively recognize my compatriots of misfortune, all those skulking survivors—by a crude tattoo, a slope of the shoulders, the hands clasped in front of the body as those of shivering addicts, a weary or furtive glance, a misfit appearance, a dead-fish quality. The ghosts, the shuffling people from some submerged Atlantis, are alive and roaming the world as if exiled from the "normal" world of prison.

◆

I am not telling you anything new, am I? How could I possibly? You would have identified the description I just gave as that of the "institutionalized" condition where "normal" life and relations exist behind the walls and not outside among the "civilians." This conditioning, by the way, I believe happens to just about everyone kept in some form of confinement or detention for more than two years. Prison *creates* prisoners. In fact, it may fabricate zombies or *model prisoners*.

It is a common fantasy among inmates that everything will come right—particularly since we are all innocent or at the very least victims of circumstances and of society—if only we could tell the warders who we *really* are, exactly what it is like seen from our side of the coin, and especially what you ought to do to shine the money and make it all work more profitably.

Prisoners have fertile though unoriginal imaginations and lots of time. We quickly learn to wag tail even as we accumulate a specific experience. You may say we become experts on the laws and customs of incarceration. Ah, we know the answer to the perennial conundrum of Crime and Punishment. Just ask us and we'll bark forever.

It does not follow, strange as it may seem, that the solutions proposed by inmates though often of the utopian variety will necessarily be less repressive. The truth is that most prisoners are morbidly fascinated, enthralled even, by prison life. I have often been struck by the fact that babies are more interested in one another than in their respective parents, the dogs walked by their masters are aware only of other dogs they cross, and prisoners passing one another in the corridors and courtyards or in the court cells seem to be oblivious of the warders escorting them. We'd soar at the chance to hiss or to smile even though we'd be punished afterwards. And I remember how in prison only news relating to our closed world would jump off the pages of the newspapers and be discussed passionately while the explosion of an atom bomb or the soggy sucking saga of a Clinton would go unnoticed.

◆

No later than last night I was asked whether prisoners hold grudges against their guards. I think not. True, in some ways our reciprocal "strangeness" may be permanently pickled in the sourness of power relations—when I arrived at the airport two days ago I was fetched and brought here in a taxi that I had to share with the head warder of an institution from some remote Caucasian republic; he spoke not a word intelligible to me, but regularly burped or farted noisily, whereupon he would swivel his head on its thick neck and look at me with a ferocious glare of disapproval and accusation ...

But we are after all of one family, are we not? We inhabit one archipelago; we live on the same premises (in fact, in most countries we will be stealing each other's food); if we get the chance we kill one another; we are cut off from the outside world by the same walls. We have to make do with one another. We are the Siamese, stuck like the prick in the arid asshole.

◆

Imprisonment has been with us ever since man started organizing communal life according to the rules of the strongest, from the time the top dog first howled. If I may digress: it is interesting how many of the basic and immemorial human activities or institutions all start with a P in English—Power, Politics, Pussy, Poetry, Prostitution, Prison, Prick ...

And since the very beginning of time there must have been warders occupying this strange and difficult and exposed and perhaps unenviable Position as the interface of the power relationship between society and those of its members considered to be beyond the Pale, however temporarily so and without regard as to how such law is written and then read. Yes, it is expected of you to be both the custodians of agreed upon norms of repression and Punishment and the agents of rehabilitation, reinsertion, and social healing. You Poor, Poor People!

I don't think it should be my task here to engage you upon the merits and the demerits of protecting society (we will keep that secret among us prisoners if you don't mind), and the equal if contradictory need to uplift the fallen individual, to get him to look at the Mountain; nor to talk about *right* and *wrong*, or the social and economic causes of crime, or cultural untranslatability, or racism, or the fundamentalist urges for revenge, or the fact that if penal conditions reflected popular wishes we'd still have capital punishment all over the world today and not just in backward and crude democracies such as the United States and China and Iran, or about the muffled sounds made by the forgotten god in his burrow.

Perhaps, I'd just briefly like to insist that you who are gathered in this august hall have by dint of your own experiences and your intimate knowledge (maybe even your incestuous knowledge) the possibility to make the larger world more aware of the texture of implications proper to penal life. Maybe you, having wiped your Penises on our underPants, can tell what the naked backside of the prisoner looks and feels like from your vantage point on the Parapets. This is more than we can say about ourselves. In many a way, dismal or otherwise, you who neither groan nor sob are the representatives, the acceptable face of us prisoners to the States, and you ought to flash your mirrors to signal that there's more to life than can be seen on the surface. Why, you may show the world that the moon is a dog!

◆

Meanwhile, here is what I want to tell *you* finally, and if I may say so from my own limited experience: There can be no chance to escape the "living death" of existence in the labyrinth except by respecting and maintaining and developing the dignity and the sense of responsibility of the individual inmate. That, and that the senses ought to be kept alive at all costs, for without antennae the shellfish are little more than bait; that family links ought thus to be encouraged; and that the prisoner must be given the chance to be gainfully employed. The most depressing aspect of being "inside" is to not be able to help your loved ones "outside."

It is the only way to break the wheel of cause and grinding. (If the intention or the better option is indeed to break it.) Or to bring out the bleeding decapitated head of the defaced or defecated one for the benefit of society. If that is what you want.

◆

P.S. *When one has had enough of prison, when one wishes to sound the retreat, one's removal can be accommodated. Simple procedures are set out on posters against the walls of the barracks: all that's needed is to report at the main gate that one intends to abscond; there one will be taken into custody and brought to the superintendent's office. Exactly an hour later, it is guaranteed, one will be executed—choked or hit behind the ear or shot or electrocuted (specifications can be negotiated)—with the official explanation acceptable to all parties that death occurred during an escape caper ... As a stranger in these parts one concentrates on learning the language. One wants to master it well so that the discourse may be effortless and impeccable on that decisive day when one has to go to the main entrance/exit. In reality, the moment of presentation will be defined entirely by one's capacity for handling the language ... It is to be surmised that the final hour in the superintendent's office, the mano a mano, eyeball to eyeball in a confined space, will be the transitional phase to a critical foreclosure. Rather like an oral examination ... What is spoken of there? This is the half-bull, half-human secret of our lives! Is this then the epiphany of closing all accounts and stopping to count? Could it be the last tilt at explanation, cracking teeth on mysteries, confession, bargaining, and justification? One then wants to have the language* inside, *to be ready and unburdened for that ultimate hour.*

Eleven

NOTES FROM THE MIDDLE WORLD

Who are you? Even when you know the answer, it is not an easy question.
—Leon Wieseltier, *Against Identity*

I'd like to taste the breeze and take a stroll through the Middle World, which is, and is not, the same as the Global Village. Let's say that those of the Middle World—I think of them as *uncitizens*, the way you have un-American activities as in contrast to those considered non- or anti-American—are Global Village vagrants, knights of the naked star. They are defined by what they are not, or no longer, and not so much by what they oppose or even reject. They ventured into zones where truths no longer fitted snugly and where certainties did not overlap, and most likely they got lost there.

In the course of doing so, proceeding by interrogation and comparison, discovering/uncovering the way and the ways of my hand, I hope to outline the territory and identify some of its inhabitants.

What I'm reaching for may be a fancy, a construct of the imagination, a conceit. I'm not even certain about the terminology. Let us rather think of it as a temporary name for what could be a passing phenomenon.

"Middle World" is probably confusing: unwittingly it resonates with "Middle Kingdom." (I'd feel more comfortable were it to evoke "the floating world" of old Japan, of actors and prostitutes and poets—though, aptly, to live in the Middle World is not unlike a long-nosed ghost living in Chinese.) In other languages, friends tell me, they find the term unsatisfactory: the French *monde du milieu* quite literally relates to the world of gangsters and politicians—not entirely inappropriate since narco-traffic, for example, like transnational business, has more of an international reach than the communion of intellectuals and artists. Carlos Fuentes, with whom I discussed the conceit, liked the notion but found the term in Spanish too wishy-washy. It may also put us in mind of Tolkien's "Middle Earth" where the hobbits live. In this instance I'd be quite delighted to accept the confusion. And there is the "Middle Passage" about which there can be no confusion, only the confounded chaos of shame; it is a process still searing the mind and a place rotting history. As for the "Middle Way," I leave that to your appreciation.

(I should stress though, that I always considered the Middle Way to be revolutionary in its close engagement with all the facets, faucets, feces, and fault lines of fleeting and flitting life.)

I call it Middle World because of its position somewhere equidistant from East and West, North and South, belonging and not belonging. Not of the Center though, since it is by definition and vocation peripheral, other, to be living in the margins and on the live edges.

(The Center, both internationally and in any given country, is always elsewhere, to the North.) Also, to be there is to be "in the middle of the world." Maybe I should push my luck and suggest we call this emerging archipelago of self-enforced freedom and unintentional estrangement partaking in equal parts of love and death, MOR. I like the sound: the land of MOR. To be among "the first of the Moricans."

(What if there were not one shared language in this world but as many tongues as you have uncitizens? And if no one could understand the other? And if the Middle World were the tower of Babel—not built upwards as the Bible imagined, for the Bible is more the projection of collective imagination than the transcription of shared memory, but down into the earth, the way Kafka intimated? What if it were no more than the area of being lost, the vacant lot of nothingness? Not to be confused with zones of nothingness-making, which is something else again—the globalization of indigence consecrating cultural consumer ethics through massive and massively pretentious and massively misleading exhibitions, destroying substance by instant universal communication slavishly and droolingly spun by vacuous pundits and media morons, blighting creative engagement by stretching television space to the outer limits of vulgarity, propagating aggressively the glad tidings that Money begetting Money through speculation is the highest good and that Capitalism as sterling moral imperative is its immaculately begotten Son/Daughter, composing elevator and shopping mall music and canning sitcom laughter, mortifying the individual conscience through rolling worldwide campaigns against hunger and slavery and for peace that will do none of these things, dulling citizen awareness by staging presidential election debates … Nothingness-making is not the upshot of Middle Worlders not having a common language; on the contrary, it is an expression of *la pensée unique*, the one language of imposed consensus and the convention of correct brainwashing. It is to attain that state that has been described by Edmond Jabès: *"You are dead. You escape the imagination."*)

My immediate purpose is not now to suggest how this space and tribe of uncitizens came into being. We are all aware of paradigm-shattering changes in the world at moments accelerating into new patterns of power. We know—have been buffeted, alienated, awed—by the cave-in of empires; we are all consumer subjects to the monopoly of a capitalist free market masquerading as "globalization of the world economy"; most of us are already caught in the tele-technological web of virtual reality and virtual knowledge and virtual communication and thus virtual imagination and virtual truth; we observe shifts in population caused by war and famine and ethnic cleansing and sometimes national liberation; despite our best commitments we probably share the *Realmoral* that makes it plausible—or is it inevitable?—to live with the now irrevocable division between rich and poor, which makes it furthermore "normal" that certain states known to be "weak" or "failed" should implode, that is, "held to consequence" by those who lord it over "the free world" (I'm thinking of Somalia, Liberia, Sierra Leone, Congo, soon Angola and Ivory Coast and perhaps Nigeria and Indonesia and Zimbabwe ...), normal too, that we should shrug our shoulders and ultimately forget these black holes.

This is not new. In one of his writings, Jacques Derrida speaks of "the first evil," the night from which so many anonymous people are struggling to emerge. He goes back to Hannah Arendt's description of *Heimatlosen*—the stateless ones, the nations of minorities and the peoples without a state (one could say the Kurds and the Palestinians of our times), and her analyses of how the principles of human rights had deteriorated. Derrida decries the erosion of "universal hospitality," that axiom Kant had considered a "cosmopolitical law."

But perhaps the situation is worse now. One may borrow Walter Benjamin's words to illustrate how, in civilized societies, police violence and intelligence control became faceless and all pervasive (*gestaltlos* and *nirgends fassbar*), as if phantoms now directed life from the shadows. Even in France, *pays des droits de l'homme*, we came close a few years ago to a proposed legal dispensation in terms of which hospitality offered to "illegal foreigners" (*étrangers en situation irrégulière*) or simply to those "without papers" (*les sans-papiers*) would have been decreed a "terrorist action."

The purpose of Derrida's text, *Cosmopolites de tous les pays, encore un effort!* (Cosmopolitans of the world, one more try!), was to explain and extol the proposal of "shelter cities" (*villes-refuges*), as in biblical times or during the Middle Ages, and to argue for its implementation.

Refuge and asylum, persecution and hospitality, indifference and difference, solidarity, home and exile—all these concepts figure in the Middle World. Tolerance and diversity, as well. In fact, to live in MOR is to promote diversity, sometimes by default. Somehow I don't think "democracy" comes into the equation and "peace" is unlikely to be on the agenda. Talking about these two notions is rather like asking Buddha whether he believes in God, when the answer was that we have here an unknowable question and why bother about what is far when we can't take care of what is near? Or should we say, with Marcel Duchamp: "If no solution, maybe no problem"?

A West African poet, Ka'afir, someone I've known on and off over the years—an outsider in Africa, a heathen among those who grovel—recently wrote to me in a letter:

> The word "peace." Ah, how voluptuous. Like "democracy." It just fills the mouth with its familiar, well-sucked, inoffensive, satisfying taste. As if one were experiencing one's own *goodness*. No indigestion, no burnt lips. It won't cause constipation and you won't grow fat on it either. In fact, it carries no nutritional connotation whatsoever. And guaranteed to have no secondary effects: it won't provoke a rash of freedom, let alone the aches of justice. Ah, "peace," "democracy," soft drugs of self-absorption—how we love to talk sweet nothings with them tucked in the cheek hard by the tongue, chew them, take them out at international conferences to lick the contours before plopping them back into the mouth ...

However much we may whistle in the dark, the Center is holding, redefining and regrouping and re-outlining, be it by Internet. Power flows there to form a stem, a spine of control. This is true for any given combination of tensions—nationally (as with cultural or religious orthodoxy), regionally, and internationally. You may wish to identify it as the One Superpower making the world safe for democracy, otherwise known as Pax Americana, or as the IMF, political correctness, the World Economic System built on the "moral" Law of History called Freedom … You may wish to name it True Faith or Jihad, which is just an unholy war, or Eretz Israel, or Hollywood, or CNN … Any number of power groupings may easily be recognized because their lowest common denominator will often be an acronym.

Did our decomposition of the Center's dicta at least help redress the iniquitous power relations between North and South? Of course not! It is true that the thought structures of Empire have long since been debunked in the colonies and the provinces, and this imparts to us a gratifying sense of being morally correct and incites us to cocky behavior. We preen and crow our equality before the Eternal, but the cock is promised for the pot and contestation has actually strengthened the hegemony: postcolonial discourse is firmly and authoritatively embedded in the syllabus of the Center's academies. Few pimps and popes are as expansively, grandly, and self-satisfyingly "understanding" and thus "accommodating" as those "iconoclasts" working in Comp. Lit. and Cultural Studies in the North. The leftist intellectuals' commitment to ambivalence, complexity, and fragmentation, to making of the penis a phallic symbol, to the death of the author and the demise of the male, and particularly to the rebuttal of "excellence," which, as it was mockingly decreed, could only be racist and pig-like—all of it originally subversive—has now led to an ideological obtuseness of decayed ethics, confusion, and the incapacity to recognize morality (since only the "self" is immoral, or rather *guilty*) or to act upon the need for solidarity.

And yet, as if in a contradictory movement, there is a surge toward cultural diversity and ethnic affirmation, perhaps in a scramble for the supposed security of self-recognition.

The margins are heaving, throwing up new ideas and old contestations, positing chaos, respecting madness. Counterforces continually emerge. In the mountains, dreamers with hoods over their heads grope for the forgotten treasure of "revolution." From the "black holes" black thoughts are vomited on paper.

And indeed, the way you are positioned to and in language may be one of the defining traits of the Middle World uncitizen. More often than not he/she will no longer be living untrammelled in the subtle regions of the birth-tongue, and memories of that "paradise" will now be travel jottings; just as often the contours of the other language(s) used will be potentially hostile shallows to be negotiated with great care and the precise circumspection of the trained orphan. But often too, these "new" spaces of self-othering will be invested with exuberance. ("And there you go again!" Ka'afir would warn me.)

Does the Middle World not also have a "ghost center"? Can there be continuing awareness outside the group, therefore beyond shared references, of a founding "loss"? Aristotle postulated that the political animal (*zôon politikon*) was not just "any old bee" but distinguished itself by a collective ethical existence. Political animals don't live in groups by instinct or only for the sake of survival and not even for the happy hell of it. No, human nature strives for more than the satisfaction of needs and desires, for lightening the skin color or finding the right lotion to darken it. Man wants to live with justice. Or used to.

For what do we still remember about the "common weal" now that our public spaces have been blighted by the barrenness of television soaps and the smirks of politicians looking for the sound bite? Do we still know and accept that the one thing we cannot be deprived of is our humanity? That, as Roger Antelme wrote after the death camps, "the SS may kill a man, but cannot change him into something else"? Isn't it this striving for transgression, transcendence, becoming other—that distinguishes us from the animals? Even when we cannot express it in words?

We seem forever incapable of grasping and expressing all the variations of our changes. The first effect of that Center which we combat or which repulses us is to stultify language, to make it "official," to substitute it for memory, to make of it the privileged means of "communication and record," thus order and authority, to repress the contestation and creativeness of uncertainty. (*"You try to be free through writing. How wrong. Every word unveils another tie,"* wrote Edmond Jabès.)

Perhaps the ideal of shared and compound and irreducible marginality I'm talking about here was best expressed in Zarathustra's favorite "center" or never-never capital called "the multihued cow," *Die bunte Kuh*. Nietzsche must have had in mind a line from an ancient Greek's verse, where the wise man is described as being one who is painted in many colors …

Is the uncitizen not just a garden-variety internationalist, perhaps a multicultured person with a hyphenated social identity? No, because you can be all of that without leaving your premises of prejudice. A Universalist, then? No, because "universal values" (as embodied in *l'homme universel*) are well understood to be Western: universalism is represented, I'd say, by a French-bound point of departure. Surely a cosmopolitan of the déclassé intelligentsia, and how does he or she differ from what used to be termed "displaced persons"? Indeed, the Middle World has affinities with all these categories, but the above terms are fairly precisely circumscribed in specific historical periods and situations.

To be of the Middle World is to have broken away from the parochial, to have left "home" for good (or for worse) while carrying all of it with you and to have arrived on foreign shores (at the outset you thought of it as "destination," but not for long) feeling at ease there without ever being "at home." Sensing too, that you have now fatally lost the place you may have wanted to run back to. Have you also lost face, or is the "original face" now unveiled? Exile? Maybe. But exile is a memory disease expressing itself in spastic social behavior: people find it a mysterious ailment and pity you greatly. (J. M. G. Le Clézio has this evocative definition of exile as "he or she who has left the island"; the ex-ile, one assumes, leaves the I-land of self to become water lapping at the continent of we-ness, of belonging.)

Exile could be a passage and you may well speak of "passage people." Yet, the Middle World is finality beyond exile. For a while at least the reference pole will remain the land from which you had wrenched yourself free or from where you were expelled. Then, exile itself will become the habitat. And in due time, when there's nothing to go back to or you've lost interest, MOR will take shape and you may start inhabiting the in-between. The terrain is rugged, the stage bathed in a dusty gray light. It is not an easy perch. Wieseltier, in another of his barbed aphorisms, says: "In the modern world, the cruellest thing you can do to people is to make them ashamed of their complexity."

One location of the Middle World is where the turfs of the outcast, the outsider, and the outlaw overlap. It could be a dominion of outers. Is it all shame, therefore? Not on your life! Listen to this poem written in the year 1080 by a Chinese world-traveler, Su Tung-p'o, a functionary who had carnal knowledge of prison and banishment:

> A hundred years, free to go, and it's almost spring;
> for the years left, pleasure will be my chief concern.
> Out the gate, I do a dance, wind blows my face;
> our galloping horses race along as magpies cheer.
> I face the wine cup and it's all a dream,
> pick up a poem brush, already inspired.
> Why try to fix the blame for troubles past?
> Years now I've stolen posts I never should have had.

(The translator, Burton Watson, adds that the third line, "I do a dance," may as well be interpreted as "I stop to piss.")

Now let me draw the line a little more clearly by proposing a very partial and partisan list of people I consider to be (or have been) of the Middle World; these well-known names make the night of the nameless ones even darker, of course.

I won't touch upon religion or science—the Dalai Lama is there by definition and Einstein was surely an uncitizen of MOR—*"I am truly a 'lone traveller' and have never belonged to my country, my home, my friends, or even my immediate family, with my whole heart; in the face of all these ties, I have never lost a sense of distance and a need for solitude ..."*; nor music (Mozart was one and so was John Cage with his glass silences), or business (I suspect that Maxwell, the news mogul who became a whale, was also an uncitizen, and Soros may well be there as philosopher pirate); nor politics (Mandela, forever driven into self-presentation by prison, burnt clean of attachments, may just be of the Middle World, Trotsky who wore round glasses and a little pointed beard in order to remember his singular self touched the black walls of this night-land, and so ultimately did Gandhi, impaled on the flash-knife of not "belonging" sufficiently) ...

You will take me to task for my choices, which depend more on feeling than verifiable assessment, but my sketchy picture includes: Kundera—for a while before he became French; Nureyev; Vidiadhar Surajprasad Naipaul—adrift while denying it; Rushdie—neither East nor West but enjoying the party immensely; Bruce Chatwin, exploring the nomadic roads all leading to death; Homi Bhabha—*"we now locate the question of culture in the realm of the beyond"*; Ieoh Ming Pei, the international architect, and so was Gaudi; Juan Goytisolo; "Saint" John of the Cross and his girlfriend, Theresa of Avilla; Yeats and Pound and Auden, but not Eliot; Eric von Stroheim, but somehow neither Dietrich nor Chaplin; Edward Said—very intermittently so; Bei Dao, the Chinese exile poet, is in the process of getting his uncitizen papers, Brecht, from the time after he returned to East Germany; Adorno who relished it, particularly in his late style; Borges—very nearly, tapping his white cane against the gates; Freud—unwittingly, which is not so strange because he fancied himself a scientist when he was in fact but an interesting writer—and probably also Jung; Samuel Beckett, who visualized the workrooms of Middle Worldliness on stage; Pessoa, populating his head with alienated explorers of the self, that slippery slope to damnation; Vladimir Nabokov, although he tried his best to dissimulate it; Joseph Conrad of the dark heart; Jean-Marie le Clézio; Henri Michaux—*"hell is the rhythm of the other"*; Rimbaud—both as poet and trader; Victor Segalen; the toothless Artaud and the mutilated Van Gogh, and Cioran who considered it a shame to have been born, and Max Ernst and Man Ray and Mayakovsky with the hole in the head, and the mild revolutionary Aimé Cesaire and Lautréamont (Isidore Ducasse), and Django Reinhard, and Primo Levi fatally drawn to the downward spiral of the dark stairwell, and Jimi Hendrix and Tristan Tzara; Leonardo da Vinci, painting backwards to the unknowable I as if to light; Faulkner going down into the thickets of language; Henry Miller, in painful lust, and his buddy, Larry Durrell; Han Shan the Cold Mountain poet and Gary Snyder his disciple; the Andalus explorers and historians; Elias Canetti; Mahmoud Darwish—*"Where should we go after the last frontiers? Where should the birds fly after the last sky?"*; Franz Fanon and Frantz Kafka; Brodsky and Walcott, angrily; Bessy Head and Amos Tutuala in their worlds of spirits; Cervantes of the Missing Hand and Goya with the Screaming Mind; Morandi and Giacometti; Carlos Fuentes but not Octavio Paz and certainly not Vargas Llosa; Frida Kahlo but not Diego Rivera; the Zapatistas of Chiapas but not the Shining Path guerrillas; Passolini but not Fellini; Ryszard Kapuscinski; Robert Walser—*"how fortunate I am not to be able to see in myself anything worth respecting and watching"*; Albert Camus; Alexandra David-Neel; William Burroughs, maybe Jack Kerouac—but, I imagine, somehow not Allen Ginsberg; the Chinese wandering monks/artists/poets/exiles; Gauguin, maybe Degas, probably Bacon with the raw meat of his thinking, and Matisse, but neither Picasso nor Cézanne nor Velasquez; Billy Holiday, but not Ella Fitzgerald; Hannah Arendt—*"I am more than ever of the opinion that a decent human existence is possible today only on the fringes of society, where one then runs the risk of starving or being stoned to death. In these circumstances a sense of humour is of great help."* And so many more down the ages …

Was Nietzsche of the detribalized tribe? Or was he more German than mad? And of his acolytes I'd include only Foucault who had the baldness and the loud taste in attire so typically uncitizen, and perhaps Deleuze, for he did sport extraordinarily long fingernails—although he gradually glad-mouthed himself back to the closed-in compulsiveness of self-indulgent French rhetoric before throwing his body like a stinking dog carcass out the window; the others (Barthes, Derrida, Kristeva) remain too rooted in a Jacobin arrogance where doubt is a cover for self-accretion, they suffer from the blindness of brilliance and besides, the text of itself (and for itself) being skein stretching over rotting body, cannot be the Middle World.

Is one always of the Middle World? It may happen, as in the case of Beckett who walked in order to fall down, and Paul Celan who never escaped, not even when he became a bloated dead goose bobbing on the oily blackness of the Seine. But one may also grow out of it. One is not normally born there, and your children cannot inherit uncitizenship.

How does one draw the map of MOR?

Wherever its uncitizens are, there the Middle World is. I don't have a complete topography because cities and countries may change their coloring on the map and the forces of conformism are voracious. Once more, I'll not argue the nuances. It should be pointed out that Middle Worlders paradoxically have a sharpened awareness of place (topoi, locus)—as with nomads, the environment may be constantly changing and one does not possess it, but it is always a potentially dangerous framework with which you must interact—and therefore they will know cloud and well and star and fire better than sedentary citizens do.

Alexandria was Middle World territory (by the way, the Middle World has nothing to do with modernity) and so was Beirut once upon a time; Sarajevo belonged before the pigs slaughtered it to "purity"; Hong Kong was an outpost (the poet, P. K. Leung wrote, in an admirable volume called *City at the End of Time*: *"Ironically, Hong Kong as a colony provides an alternative space for Chinese people and culture to exist, a hybrid for one to reflect upon the problems of a 'pure' and 'original' state"*); Paris used to be a section of MOR when it still had a proletariat, many of whom were of foreign origin, living within the walls (by the way, the Middle World has nothing to do with riches or urban sophistication); Cuba may be of the Middle World despite its best efforts at being communist; Berlin, still, although it is now becoming "normalized" as the pan-Germanic capital; Jerusalem, even though its present rulers try to stamp it with the seal of fanatic exclusivity; South Africa went through the birth pains, it was close to understanding a cardinal Middle World law—that you can only survive and move forward by continuing to invent yourself—but then it became a majority-led and -smothered democracy instead; New York, except when it is too close to America; I have heard tales of tolerance and center-insouciance from a town once known as Mogador, now Essaouira; Tangier, where I celebrated my twenty-first birthday (birdday) wrapped in a burnoose, was a refuge despite the closed warren of its Casbah; Timbuktu—how could I forget that sand-whispering place, and the other holy sites of books that could only be reached on the swaying backs of camels—Chinguetti, Ouadane, Tichit and Oualâta; Gorée, Sal, Lamu, Zanzibar, Haiti, and the other Caribbean islands—most islands tend to be natural outcrops of MOR; Palestine most certainly—"exodus" can be a high road to the Middle World, and what is now termed the Territories (a euphemism for ghettos and Bantustans, subject to Apartheid) will breed a new generation of uncitizens.

There could be areas of Middle Worldness that are socially defined, separate and specific, perhaps temporary, drifting through the surrounding waters of belonging like ice floes ultimately melting: I'm thinking of that long middle period when mentally disturbed people are "cured" and have to learn the vocabulary and the codes of a "normal" world, where one audited fiction must now take precedence over the other "deviant" one; and feminists who broke away from rules and values imposed by the patriarchy to reinvent their lives freed from the shackles of family and decorum, and who may do so until the bitter end of purdah and pariah loneliness; and "rehabilitated" prisoners becoming invisible while carrying with them an inner universe of extreme humiliation where isolation bounces off steel and concrete; and societies gutted by war and self-war that have to rebuild around the ruins of brutally destroyed "normalcy."

What are the further characteristics of a Middle World resident?

It is important to know that being of the Middle World is neither romantic nor does it imply a value. The uncitizen may well have a number of negative affinities and certainly he or she will bristle with contradictions. He will have a conflicted relationship to identity—perhaps mourning the loss of its essence while multiplying the acquisition of other facets.

Culturally such a person will be a hybrid. (*"Purity is the opposite of integrity."*—Wieseltier) This is both a precondition and a consequence. Is the bastard more tolerant? Not sure. There could be greater understanding, yes, because he ought to have "natural access" to the different strains of his makeup. (I'm using the male pronoun generically.) But often the hybrid is very persnickety in the itemization of grades of distinction. Such a person may be inordinately aware of categories.

The Middle World person has a vivid consciousness of being the Other, and is probably proud of it. Jenaro Talens wrote: *"Yo soy él que ocupa el mismo lugar que yo."* (I am he who occupies the same space as I.)

At heart he will be a nomad and he will practice nomadic thinking, even if he doesn't move around much. The best-seasoned nomads are those who never travel.

In any given country s/he will be a Southerner.

As an artist he will practice an inventive and transforming reporting of fact, using the self ("identity") as a transient and mutating guest in his work: he was there, he knows it can never be the way it is remembered.

He also knows it is the *matter* of making that establishes the Middle World as a means to that consciousness of alienation from which he cannot escape. In other words, it will be by crossing lines and exploring the contours that the artist discovers and "creates" the Middle World, which will generate his separateness.

For he will be obliged to create concepts: the security of repeating the known is forbidden to him, and this is why fundamentalists of all stripes will abhor and wish to expectorate the very name.

The processes of metamorphosis and the evolution of change will still fascinate him when yardstick and purpose are lost. James Joyce ended up living in MOR.

S/he is superstitious: all gods must be placated and survival is a question of nurtured luck.

Culture is a matter (the matter) of food, drinking sessions, markets, street life, theaters, clubs, and he may well have a keen interest in clothes. (Even Einstein's dishevelled appearance may have been a studied look.) He is less attracted to conference halls and academies.

He will assiduously exercise the necessary art of being invisible among the poor but will have scant patience with bureaucrats and culturocrats. He will also have no loyalty to the state although he may sometimes pretend to in order to embarrass the authorities of the day. Patriotism is like God, a concept much too distant, too bluntly animal and too cruel for useful contemplation.

He will be attached to fetishes. The chameleon and the parrot are emblems.

To him (her) the form—more correctly, the posture—is as important as the contents. He will learn the Oriental way, by mimesis. There is as much mysticism in light and in surface as there is in darkness.

Role-playing may be significant, appearances matter a lot, the personality will be split so as to cover all bases and accommodate all comers. Consciousness, even when it is centered, is multiple. Considerations of "bourgeois honesty" are secondary. When you're blind you don't know what "straight ahead" means.

Whether or not he is a criminal is not important; the world of thievery and honor may well be his environment of predilection—as it was for Jean Genet, a prime protagonist of Middle World uncitizenship.

He will inhabit the *nada* and have a lifelong intimate dialogue and affinity with death.

He will recognize likenesses with other Middle Worlders and there may well be a code of sharing.

A central question remains: how do we, as a species of intelligence (that is, of projecting backward and forward hypotheses of invention, the experience of memory and of imagination) and of self-reflexive fancy— by allowing these hypotheses then to define us among other intelligent life-forms (no life without change and a measure of adaptation in the will to endure, therefore no life without intelligence)—how do we see/ invent ourselves? Perhaps we are at last abutting on the outer boundaries of sequential thinking, the Cartesian folly that the mind is logical with the perceivable world outside conforming to the laws of the mind, and the Copernican angst which decided that the geometrical description of the trajectory of planets was not make-believe but true—these positions whence flowed the arid arrogance of "progress" and "conquest" with the last shudders constituted by those protagonists of the autonomy of language, of "creating and knowing by naming," who hold to the primacy of text or discourse, the deconstructionists who were so homo-infatuated they believed the outlaw mind could be in-lawed, that a flaw was but an imperfect or flubbed law. They subscribed only to the thrust for power of Nietzsche's will and autonomy of language and conveniently

forgot about the breakdown. They thought that a pattern surmises control which can be subsumed in laws and that these construct reality; they
forgot to forget themselves, forgot as well that perception (through language) is itself a narrative—of necessity using all the tricks of invention
(repetition, likeness, believability …), not to mention what it chooses
to see/perceive/recognize and what it would rather ignore or twist, and
mistaking itself, as it must, for "reality." Wasn't it Ronald Reagan, the
Great Communicator, that masterful deconstructionist (or destroyer?),
who claimed that reality is but an illusion that could be overcome? How
do we go about not losing the sense of loss?

If, as I claim, the opposite is true, if the narrative is but a shadow
of the *nada*—with all the creative potential and beauty of illusion and
invention, and if we are constantly defined and undefined by the narrative of self-invention, by the ultimate joy of nothing-making—on
what must we then base our moral conduct?

To be of the Middle World is to be aware of the moral implications
of narrative, to know and respect the knowledge that we are all part
of the same nothing. It is to "know" about the power and the limits
(and the fugacity) of self-invention, and that the ultimate power is non-
power. Of course, it can be shown that our nothings are vastly different
and also subject to perception, that our words and silences grow out
of our relationship with a personal nothing that we may think to be
general. (*"In silence, we always eavesdrop on death."* —Edmond Jabès.)
The Middle World is (ideally?) where the nothingness of being and the
being of nothingness are continually inflected by the ethical awareness
of living in a society where you are responsible through the narrative
for others, and by the sharpened imperative of non-power—which
should not be equated with the static. From an accrued sensitivity
to the rapport between words (the *narrative*) and action (*movement*)

Middle World ethics arise.

I'm leaving many stones unturned here. Perhaps just as well because we don't necessarily know what to do about the scorpions and the spiders. Among these stones there would be: What privileges, if any, come with the territory? Does the uncitizen define his moral parameters? Will the emerging shared ethic be new or is the Morican but an old-fashioned humanist at bay? Is there really honor among thieves? Since moral awareness is rooted in language, what happens to the polyglot? How does the Middle Worlder use his native tongue? Can he still have one, or is he tongue-tied like Man Friday? Can she or he be a native of anywhere? What are the uses of language to her or to him? (In *Les Mots*, Sartre suggested that one *speaks* in one's native tongue but *writes* in a foreign language.)

If awareness is movement, where does he or she think he's going, she's going—or doesn't it matter? Will it be deeper inward or outward toward others, or always both at once? If past and present are one seamless whole (the white hole of becoming), if you live in the possible tense, if you think of the past as destroyed time—what happens to memory? (And you know that time, which inexorably becomes the "past," can never be destroyed, and exactly for that very reason; it is alive and ever-elusive, moving in and out of the light. *"Death is the past that persists."* —Edmond Jabès) Should anything *happen* to memory? If you keep on inventing and multiplying yourself—whose memory do you ultimately mix with the soil?

In the manual of divination, called *The Book of Mutations*, we find descriptions of "non-changing mutation" (the original Void), "simple mutation" as of stars and moons and words, and the "changing mutation" of human life. For a person, time would follow a double course: the linear changing mutation toward where the old bitch, *la chingada*,

Death, waits with twitching tail to relieve time of all anxiety; and life's circling to unchanging mutation. Interaction and the relationship man-world were expressed in two terms: *ch'ing*, meaning "inner feeling," and *ching*, meaning "exterior landscape."

What happens to the identity that you used as a white walking stick along the way, the one you used to beat back Dog? Walking on, crossing the lines into the Middle World, is at once a way of being divested of self and creating self. Perhaps differently. Maybe another one—"maybe I was everyone," Paul Celan remarked—as a line of observation and forgetting. That too will pass, and pass away. *"I will also send the teeth of beasts upon them, with the passion of the serpents of the dust,"* Jan van Eyck wrote under one of his more apocalyptic paintings. Against the background of the unchanging, *the lines* can define, call forth, enclose a future of exclusion and extinction.

The stratagems? Paul Celan wrote: "you climb out of yourself forever." And as well: "There will be something, later, / which fills itself with you / and heaves itself / into a mouth." Rimbaud, outlawed like Gauguin and Nietzsche, prophesied the "doubling of self." His was that modern revolt, modernist even, that led to a kind of liberation. He'd postulate: *"la vraie vie est absente"* (true life is absent)—always the pulling power of what's not there—while making a kingdom of the one he envisioned in its place. And yet, he too grew silent and submitted to the rhythm of the unchanging. Or was his exploration of the Horn of Africa, once he'd vomited out the worm of words from the mouth, just poetry in action, further adventures in the double (and thus troubled) field of the Real and the Imaginary? *"Thank God this life is the only one,"* he wrote toward the end, *"and that there's no other, since it is impossible to imagine a more lamentable one."*

Leaving the I of exile, crossing the lines, is a way of exploring expanding understanding when the pap of received dogma can no longer nourish the mind; it is the road of opposition, of subversion, of "truth" in the making/unmaking process of metamorphosis, of revolution, of working with unthinkables, of living in the *possible tense*—to end up in the Middle World.

It is to live in that part of consciousness where stains will not go away, where history is a reminder of the horrors of the state of man and imagination is as strong as history—indeed, where memory and imagination are alive and interacting to transform one another; that zone where you are neither victim nor refugee and guilt is left behind for the dog of death to gnaw on (although accountability remains stuck in the throat); where you become an active protagonist of your own life, using it as a line to cross; where you will be a travelling salesman of nothingness, without self-pity but with compassion.

I have no doubt that what I describe here has become a prominent condition of that *position* where, as bastard offspring of the state and sons-and-daughters-of-many-struggles and runaway slaves of historical determinism, we must and still can outlive ourselves as the happy bums of the global village (now on fire).

I'm done. But I cannot conclude without tipping a hat to a true ancestor of the Middle World, Constantin Cavafy, the Alexandrian poet of Greek extraction who died in 1933. He it was who famously wrote: "And now, what's going to happen to us without barbarians? They were, those people, a kind of solution."

Well, we know now he need not have worried, since we are still here.

In his fine introduction to his equally excellent translation of Cavafy's poems, Edmund Keeley perceptively celebrates the uncitizen's Alexandrian myth, talking of "the virtues of historical perspicacity, of seeing things not only for what they are but what they are likely to become, including the inevitable reversals in history that finally teach one not so much the moral as the tragic sense of life ... the virtues of irony ..."

One should indeed (as Cavafy reminds us through Keeley), keep the soul open to those things that satisfy the spirit and the body: beautiful lovers given to sensual pleasures, imaginative creations of various kinds, mixed cultures and mixed faiths, the value of both art and artifice, of spectacle, of politic theater—so that the soul may carry within it the ripening prospect of its own death, but also so that the day's work may show there's no other life worthy of celebration.

May we thus learn to taste and appreciate the salt of our existence from Cavafy's "commitment to hedonism, to political scepticism, and to honest self-awareness ... (to) judgment suspended and mercy granted, though not to the viciously power hungry, or puritanically arrogant, or the blindly self-deceived."

Twelve

OF CAMELS AND DOGS AND RATS WHEN
WALKING THE WORDS / STAGING THE SELF

Or: What it Is Like to Live with Somebody
Very Much Like Myself

Essays, like butterflies, jazz (and God), move irregularly, not linearly.
—Edward Hoagland

Chögyam Trungpa writes in *The Heart of the Buddha*: "In Buddhism, mind is what distinguishes sentient beings from rocks or trees or bodies of water. That which possesses discriminating awareness, that which possesses a sense of duality—which grasps or rejects something external—that is mind. Fundamentally, it is that which can associate with an "other"—with any "something" that is perceived as different from the perceiver. That is the definition of mind. The traditional Tibetan phrase defining mind means precisely: 'That which can think of the other, the projection, is mind.'"

Dear Reader, I suspect what you really want me to talk about if I were to be true to the heading, at least in its implications of being elsewhere, would be on a topic such as, maybe, "Theater and Exile." Let us then walk around it, for talking is also to be taking the mind for a walk with memory as shadow in the ground. But surely, such an assignment must present an oxymoron. All theater, I'd venture to say is the setting and the staging of exile.

To the extent that it is holding up a mirror to society, playing out and thus shaping the tragedy and the comedy of our lives and our lines, giving voice to the dark scream of being or to the rushing silences of the turbulent stream that will take us under the ground, and we do this so as to make these moments magical or, on the contrary familiar, and thus to counteract their innate force—to this extent theater performs the tasks of exile. That is, both to stand back and to bring closer. To give sight to the "blindness" of normal, integrated living by sharpening our awareness of the problematical position of the observer, the alienation that positioning implies, by alerting us to the distance between the observer and the events he or she looks at, and then by making us look at those events and situations with a non-belonging eye. To be in exile is to have your life played out before your eyes, the recurrent memories now becoming encapsulated movements and rituals, and the dreams a flapping reel of fantasies. This space or rift between "you" and "it" is one of language and gesture, of repetition, of directing the lights to illuminate and isolate the cherished moments and the traumatic breaks. This distance between you and *it*, you sense, is the stream of consciousness you have to cross to get back to the oblivion of the normal dead. The curtain is a sheet of fire on no-man's-land, a frontier to the suspension of space and time. Another "reality" then, like our daily one, but now with the skin stripped away.

I'm going to quote Deleuze who had this to say about Nietzsche in an essay called "L'éclat de rire de Nietzsche":

> That which goes without saying for Nietzsche is that society cannot be the last call. The last instance is creation, art: or rather, art represents the absence and the impossibility of a final instance. From the very outset of his oeuvre Nietzsche posits that there are reasons 'a little higher' than those of state or society. His whole oeuvre is cast in a dimension that is neither

historical, even if we understand this dialectically, nor eternal. This new dimension that is both in time and acting against time, he calls the *untimely* or the *unseasonable*. That is where life as interpretation has its source.

Now, I can turn the proposition around and say exile is an act of theater. You know what I mean: there is the learning of lines, the props used to create the illusion of reality, the makeup through which you escape or enhance the self, the playing of roles and the imitation of the other to the point of inhabiting him or her, the invention of a past to be convincing in a place where there is only the present, the good nights and the bad ones but somehow you're always on the road and the show must go on, the empty halls into which you shout, the chronic lack of money, the rubber swords and the ketchup blood and the superstitious tears, the self-dramatizing through glycerine tears and the ham acting. But also the working knowledge that declaiming and projecting your life is both to perpetuate and link it to the fleetingness of the moment, and that the contents of understanding (perhaps even of belonging) will come through the unquestioned imitation of outer forms. That ultimately the stage flooded by the dust of light will be heaven and death.

Reader, what I present here is neither structured essay nor even a coherent paper; rather think of it as a walkabout during which I'm attempting to lay down the songlines of my meandering thoughts. To say, "lay down" is also to discover. Everything has been said since the beginning and we only uncover different portions to mull over from time to time as we stop to look at the stars or the clouds by day, and trace their racing shadows over the earth. Walking creates its own landscape like an unfolding text or a banner signalling the sound of marching feet. Because I'm the one doing the walking I will naturally imagine that I am responsible for the changes I see around me. From *here* to *there* I will stop and be surprised at the way things—that is, sentences stuffed with

the motion of words—flutter and fit together in unexpected combinations, or fall apart to show the emptiness behind all appearance. Perhaps
I will wish to share the surprises and the impressions with somebody
very much like myself, and hence with you as reader.

I am not exactly the most intelligent person to be conversing with.
Although I know how to sweet-talk as well as the next suspect, you will
not learn much. Let's walk on nevertheless, to where words are light in
the wind. Of course we can go very far, right up to where time will stop
us in our tracks, but for now we'll cleave to the shadow trotting along
between my feet. I am, after all, projecting my darkness on the stage.

Sometimes, when I'm alone for long stretches I watch my self, this
other, going through the motions of living. It happened not all these
many months ago over an extended period in and near Mother City
(Cape Town). My wife, Golden Lotus, was far away in Vietnam and I
had to make all the choices, feed and clothe myself, and in general deal
with the world. There were moments when I knew what the other was
doing; I saw the many mistakes in his awkward or arrogant interaction
with people, the limp he was showing off, and his waste of time. It was
no use remonstrating because he is a headstrong fellow (as so many
weak and vain people are) and he has always preferred hustling and
trusting his lucky star rather than reason in order to regain a semblance
of social balance. Then there followed long hours when he was opaque
to the world: I'd watch him from the corner of my eye and it would be
as if he were dead; it was impossible to tell if anything was going on
in his head. At most I'd hear him making up silly rhymes about the
spectacular scenery through which we so often drove. Was he bored?
Or just at a loss? Was he trying to impress *me*?

> Will the heart then not leap
> with glee when looking upon the beauty

of these blue-red mountains?
Is it possible to remain silent,
not to sing until voice disintegrates
in the pale expanses of utter emptiness?

At other moments, I was indeed suitably impressed by some deft reaction that gave the impression of native intelligence at work. From Mother City he ("I," more precisely "we") traveled via Paris to Gorée Island and all of a sudden we found ourselves—remember?—in a more hectic situation where a host of decisions had to be made in rapid succession, also involving the movements of other people. I watched him trying to be wise, I even seconded him or twitched a facial muscle to remind him of precedents he experienced elsewhere in the practice of his art of being intimate with strangers, of the conceivable implications; in short, how not to raise the wrong sail, at least not with a mistaken face nailed to the mast. At night I helped him find a friendly mirror; then I'd look at him, wink and cluck my tongue sympathetically. The most I can say in our defense is that we managed to keep our cool. The ceiling fans helped. (You will bear this out.)

I already said walking is another story. (Like Alice falling into memory-imagination, recognizing the I is exactly to be embarking upon another story.) *You* are asking questions as we pause to observe the environment, the page with its disturbed ant colony of letters, passing yourself off as my beautiful Reader looking to enter upon a dialogue with me, and this "other" will do his best to answer—perhaps smirking at the mirror. I'll leave the two of you to it.

You say my work is too often marred by obscenities, betrayal, pornography, hate, estrangement, disillusionment, and dead dogs floating in the gutters. True, but such an assessment is not the subject of the paper we're unfolding here and now; it is my firm intention to look for the neutral ground of a stage over which we may dance. I will grant though, you say, that exile and associated identities of the drifter, the nomad and the outsider feature prominently in my writing. That I often use these motifs to evoke a state I describe as inhabiting the "Middle World." Could I elaborate on this notion of identity and what exactly it implies?

True, as well. In an essay written some time back, "Notes from the Middle World," I tried to suggest that the concept (and it is actually also a physical location) is an emerging archipelago somewhere beyond exile. Exile, I want to remind you, is to be dwelling in a state of waiting for the changes in regime that would permit you to return to the place where origin is rooted; it is also a way of life defined by your relationship to that lost paradise, a behavior very often made stuffy and somber by successive seizures of inconsolable self-pity.

(In Spanish the word for "exile" is *destierro*: to be *desterrado*, "de-earthed," to have lost your footing—or is it to be brought up as a corpse?)

The Middle World, on the other hand, inhabited by us bums of the Global Village, is the position of *being* on your way to the vacuous, for you can neither return to where you came from nor will you ever be integrated to the point of unconscious belonging in the place you fled to for asylum. Perhaps I should say it is the *process* of being neither fish nor fowl. In a way it heralds the end of exile, but to accede to the Middle World it is not necessary to have been geographically displaced: Kafka, I pointed out, lived there even though he never really left Prague.

You could, if you want to, explore this no-where place as a labyrinth. Willem Boshoff, a Fuck-land artist, in a paper called "Notes Towards a 'Blind' Aesthetic," makes the point that the labyrinth as blind device cuts the hoodwinked or blindfolded explorer off from visual contact with other certainties, and actually signifies the essential mission of finding some *self* in the center. The cardinal function of the maze would then be to make the core or the heart impenetrable. Reaching and breaching the center becomes an initiation into sanctity and absolute reality. On your way there, crawling on your knees (Boshoff suggests), memory committed and spliced to prayer will be the string of redemption. (Or would it be a rope?)

Now, you and I know that the *self* is a Minotaur—an anguished, bellowing, monstrous beast, the offspring of coupling between human and animal and therefore forever in the raging pain of questions that cannot find answers—whose head must be chopped off and brought out into the light for the city to live in peace. The sun bull is so black with rage that you cannot look it in the face. You need a mirror. Theseus' memory, a ball of recollective string, you may remember, was held in the grasp of Ariadne. You follow this thread until you reach the anchor, the moon, to be liberated forever from the maddening reflections bobbing on the waves. The convolutions of the labyrinth, the mists and miasma clouding the path and making the passes so cold, are therefore proposed as the female saving force. So that you may say, "The labyrinth is a kind of Paradise regained, attaining realization after ordeals, a knot to be untied in the dark." (It is rather bracing to think of the maze as a woman.)

But the Middle World, as I see it, is not a maze and neither is it Paradise. You are not strung along. It is not lost and you are no longer in exile there; it is a place coming into founding, heaving into sight. And it is certainly not of the Center, at least not in political and social terms. The inhabitants there, practicing multiple identities, may be nowhere—as I proposed, in the "middle of the world,"—but they are still acutely aware of being on the go. They are also, paradoxically, keenly aware of *place*, and will have developed peripheral vision just as they practice parallel thinking. It is the only way you can perceive of the beauty and the danger of birds. When you dangle from the end of a rope you will want to know these things.

This sense of place will emerge from "the interplay between geography, memory and invention in the sense that invention must occur if there is recollection," as Edward Saïd pointed out in his essay, "Palestine: Memory, Invention and Space." He then further underlined "the extent to which *the art of memory* (my italics) for the modern world is both for historians as well as ordinary citizens and institutions very much something to be used, misused and exploited, rather than something that sits inertly there for each person to possess and contain." Memory only exists when it is deployed, and then it is an artwork.

Let me sidle up to this shifting perception from another angle. Under "normal" circumstances, born and bred and ultimately buried or cremated in a stable environment—it will always be untimely—in an old country where you know the earth under your fingers like a cemetery, in a "mature democracy" as it is nowadays called—in these circumstances, the sense of self is a given, and often it goes unquestioned. Your grandfather would have known your name. In exile, on the other hand, there's a heightened awareness of the self having become a suspended frozen identity, a hovering dog waiting to be allowed back in the yard. Dog may well be man's best friend laughing a red tongue, but it whimpers at night as it licks its paws for some recollection of lost tracks. In the Middle World, that self will be scattered like confetti at the wedding of the knave and the bull. To get there you probably walked over the burning coals of exile. Fire consciousness is a notion enhancing the dissolution of self, the dismantling of a fixed identity, and yet it is also part of the Tao or the Watercourse Way.

What is the "I" then if the stable self no longer exists? You will become aware of being of a "bastard race" (to quote Rimbaud), to be living in a "minor language," to be a theater rat. The I would have been diffused in a sharpened alertness to patternmaking. Not only are you an uncitizen, but more than likely also as nonpatriotic as a parrot. And so you will be seen to be, depending on your inclination or perhaps just the time of day: the clown, the hermaphrodite, the border intellectual, the bastard, the heretic, the outsider, the shaman, the fly in the ointment, the dunce, the cockroach, the underling, the nomad, the smuggler, the mirror, the chameleon. You will also be your own ancestor and your own landscape. You will be patterned movement toward the absurdity of death, which is the extinction of consciousness, with decay the dissolution of patterns. Don't turn back now, and admit that even love and hate are no longer feelings but only affects! As the self becomes a deterritorialized velocity of affects unleashing it, feelings will be spewed from the interior of a "subject" to be projected violently outward into a milieu of pure exteriority. That scattered self, flakes from the smoking pyre, ejaculated seed, will surface in relays, intermezzos, and resurgences. The self, I'm telling you, is a rhizome and a war machine (to talk with Deleuze and Guattari) inhabiting the "smooth" space of the nomadic way as opposed to the "striated" space of the state. And here we have the confrontation looming through the mists of mad metaphor: Self, which is Middle World, against State, which is Center or Unum God.

Beyond the labyrinth where everything has existed since all time—dogs and minotaurs and lovers and emptiness and moon and handkerchiefs and blood and howling and Africa and freedom and laughing trees and eclipses and memorized imagination, which is imagined memory—a form is struggling to take shape. Form cannot exist without expression. Expression flows from movement. Movement gives birth to stillness. Stillness represents absent movement. A line is born: the navel string of decay

traced in pencil lead. Coffins are lined with the black lead of writing the
surroundings, which eventually will digest the content.

Watch me as I now briefly turn around with the ball of string in my
hand to return to where we started out, and observe how I do not fall
over myself despite my advanced age. You see, the labyrinth, the theater
space, is actually associated with movement. I told you it was a woman,
didn't I? One could say, as I did at the outset of our walk, that you shape
the road in the process of walking. One walks to get lost. Isn't that the
only pleasure left? The nomad's space of development has to become an
inner one, a plain of immanence over which one moves on the way to
death. This is of course an image where thought encapsulates itself and
is staged.

Understanding will unclothe the image or even meaning: it cannot be
fixed. It moves against the dullness of information. It is movement, it is
metaphor. It is detonation. The aim is not to survive, but to keep one step
ahead of the deadening hand of the state of reasonable understanding. To
keep moving the image must set off resonance …

Feet dancing the earth may well be more important than memories. Or could it be argued that for the nomad memory dwells in the
feet? As the hollow-eyed ones paint the walls of their caves or huts,
so they also daub their bodies. These marks will not express ideas but
exult processes and passages. And as in Zen, you will find no manuals
and no teaching worth a burp, just the acquiring of some inner sight
through the imitation of outside movements made ageless by time.
You keep imitating movement in order to find the *form.* The surface
remains an impenetrable mystery, a skin for the patterns of migration
through time. We are back in the skin trade!

Naturally, as you acquire so too you discard. At what point do we
come *together*? There is no blueprint for how social organizations will

be constructed. By "organization" one should understand a continual process of composition and decomposition. In the Middle World all uncitizens are equal, and such a horizontal society will be the open site, the Fresh Kills that fosters practical creation and composition, destruction and decomposition. New patterns will surface. Marx well understood that the living force of society continually emerges from the spent powers of the social order: living labor refuses to be sucked dry by the vampires set in flight by capitalism.

I'll sum up. The nomadic notion is a movement of variations, an ambulant territorial idea and a deed where the body itself, liberated from the constraints of a fixed I, becomes a terrain-shifting landscape. Now, we are confronted by a political consciousness growing from this network of becoming. Herein the nomadic art and the ever-wandering range of aesthetic perceptions will assume an anarchical stance against the stratified order of father and state. The revolutionary body will be plucked from the earth, de-earthed from the burial tombs of Che Guevara and Steve Biko and Frantz Fanon to be carried along as talismanic bones of the ancestor to be thrown so as to show the way. Why? "The goal of revolution is transformation," Gary Snyder said. But we'll have to be patient like the chameleon walking over the surface of the mirror if we wish to capture the image.

One must learn the slow art of revolutionary patience. One has to explore subterranean tracks, find the graves of stars, the hidden rivers surfacing as eyes elsewhere, in another history. The writer/painter must acquire frontier consciousness.

Now, why are you winking like that at me in the mirror? Or are you wincing? Because the hot air I spout, quoting myself to boot, is misting over the image? I agree, one should not be blinded by over-indulgence.

You speak of mirror—maybe as the immanent field of change you had in mind? I know the mirror as powerful metaphor of identity can be traced throughout art and writing. Perhaps one just has a mortal fear of losing face! In my play (*Die Toneelstuk/The Play*), it would appear that the many selves mirror our multiple identities, but then it goes on to also confront the viewer with a real mirror-as-prop to include him/her in the transmutations of the characters on stage. I'll confess here that the play intended to offer a provocative social commentary on a futile collective attempt at self-retribution for past wrongs. Yet, you point out, those mirrored identities perversely imply exactly that—a *one for all* and *all for one* sense of shared responsibility, not only in South Africa, this poor country I so facetiously sneer at as Fuck-land, but also for all the wrongs ever committed in the whole world. Your alter ego *Baba Halfjan*, then parodies this statement or attitude you say. Am I correct to assume that responsibility, if that is what it is, springs anyway from our shared identity as human beings (and hence the futility of self-flagellation, for we're all born in the same shit), and if so, could you please elaborate? Also, specifically in the above context of social accountability, whether I experience the creative act as social gesture? (As well—I can hear you think—will you please speak less densely and allusively and cut out all the unnecessary and mostly stolen crappy references to the ruminations of abstract theoreticians with long nails and dirty hats? One has trouble following you through the labyrinth.)

(Whereas I thought we were not doing so badly! But I'll try my best.)

Achluophilia or the love of darkness, you may know, is not always coupled with an aversion to looking. But it is true that many sighted ones fear the day they will not be able to see and therefore they are also afraid of the dark. "For now we see through a glass darkly ..." (I apologize—I'm quoting the sun bull.) Excavations have shown first-century glass to be very impure; thus its turbid opaqueness was well suited to express the metaphor of the body being the dark medium of spiritual vision. The "dark glasses" of scripture are revealed as a mirror, its clarity delayed in time ("but then shall I know even as also I am known"). Mirroring is of course an autobiographical way of looking at the other. Whereas dark glasses are associated with lost virginity in popular iconography, the mirror as unbroken looking glass will denote intact virginity. Go figure! You see, mirror symbolism is one of thesis and antithesis. Like the echo, the looking glass stands for twins. Lewis Carroll surely intended for Alice's soul to free itself by passing through the mirror to the other side and to resurface there on the stage of a packed theater. Weren't actresses supposed to have loose morals? The "darkly"that we find in the biblical text was translated from the Greek; experts tell us that "enigma" or "riddle" would have been the closer translation. Fearing and finding ourselves in art, like the blind pilgrims in their labyrinth, is enigmatically coupled to the vaguely reflective illusion we have of ourselves in the present. It can be hard to take this knowledge. That is why, on occasion, we must cover up the mirror and turn it face to the wall so that looking at themselves may not transfix the dead. It could well be that we need thus to cloud the elements of finding and losing, of clarity and obscurity, of feeling and *feeling* (touch), of seeing with eyes and *seeing* through closed eyelids, in order to rediscover our own redemptive blindness. Is the only solution not to bury the mirror? What happens under the ground, the images born there, I don't know. Maggots and worms will sort that one out ...

Forget it. Now, to return to the social ramifications you ask about: Was it not Sartre who proclaimed that the *word* is an *act*? I remember reading how very upset Vargas Llosa was when Sartre later prescribed that Third World writers should put fine writing aside to become the pen-carriers of revolution in their countries. *What*, he fulminated, *was the word as act no longer sufficient?* Are we to be stripped of our multi-hued coats? We are luckily no longer there any-more, revolution is a distant echo of thunder over misty hills, and so not really pressed into forced idealism—except perhaps in countries like Afghanistan and Iraq and Bhutan. And, for not unlike reasons, in Mr. Bush's America.

The creative act as displacement or extension of consciousness al-ways has social resonance. It is an intervention provoking interaction with the environment in which we all live—social, political, cultural, or physical—even when confined to its page or space of inception. Deeper than that still, the creative gesture relates to the rhythm, the flow, and the breaks of the primordial movements and spaces, to the need to placate and exorcize and escape and imitate underlying all shared human consciousness. We create because we have this urge to multiply and re-invent and share ourselves. This is an underground movement.

In Jean Genet's *Un captif amoureux* I found the following (my own writing as echo is just a distant mulling and mumbling of what he did so splendidly):

> When man composes an image which he wants to propagate, which he may even wish to substitute for himself, he searches, he makes mistakes, he drafts aberrations, any number of non-viable monsters, images of himself that he should tear up if they didn't come undone by themselves: it is because finally, the image that will remain after the withdrawal or after death must be active (*agissante*) ... Theater may well disappear in its present worldly form—already, it would seem, it is under threat—but the theatrical remains constant if by that we understand the need to propose

not signs but complete and compact images dissimulating a reality that is perhaps an absence of being. The void. So as to bring about the definitive image which he wishes to project into that future as absent as his present, every man is capable of definitive acts that will topple him into nothingness.

And as an illustration earlier in the same book, Genet has Saint-Just declaring—this comes just after Fouquier-Tinville sentenced him to the guillotine, when fleeing to not lose his head to the mirror of blackness was still an option: "I despise this dust I'm made of and which now speaks to you, but nobody can wrench from me this independent life that I gave myself through the ages to come, and in heaven." [A Dutch poet, Kees Stip, wrote: *"Miljarden jaren ben ik dood geweest, en ik leef nog geen eeuw of het is alweer zo."* (Billions of years I've been dead and I'm hardly alive for a century when it is time again.)]

The mirror in the play you talk about can be seen as the physical location where transformation becomes visible. The book written by the writer, for instance, is a mirror. Why, it even talks back! This one I'm working on at present, is titled: *MOR: The Mirror as Memory of the Middle World.* What a fuck-up! Jorge Luis Borges ascribed to his compadre, Bioy Casares, a celebrated phrase: *"Los espejos y la cópula son abominables, porqué reproducen el número de los hombres."* (Mirrors and copulation are abominable because they multiply the number of people.) Is that why there are so many people on the earth?

Let me strip the image and propose that the creative act ideally should be ethical—naked as I suggested earlier, in order to be as close as possible to "truth" in experience and observation and thereby carry its recognition and acceptance of responsibility. However, it may not necessarily conform to our constructs and discourses of public morality. In fact, so as to be effective (that is, to heighten the awareness of textures) it will probably challenge those comforts.

Shitao, the Chinese ink master who lived from 1642 to 1707 of the modern era, wrote in his treatise, *Words on Painting of the Monk "Bitter Pumpkin"*: "Everything that has constant rules must of necessity also have variable modalities. If there's a rule, there must be change. Starting from knowledge of the constants, one may begin modifying the variables; as soon as you know the rules, you have to start transforming them. (…) Nature has given me everything; and so, when I study the ancients, why can't I transform them?"

Isn't he also saying that we all have "human nature," which is the life we share, but that this will always be sullied by conventions prescribed by the powerful and that we thus have to constantly rethink our attitude and approaches to the codified expressions of our communal consciousness?

Did those of us who worked in the pumpkin patch of that simultaneously promised and doomed land—I'm now referring specifically to Fuck-land, South Africa—really shift the boundaries of perception and understanding? We were free to do so now, not so? True, we had all come a long way since the dead times of Apartheid. But, begging your indulgence and without meaning to demean any of the achievements or real gains for a majority of people under the new regime, it will be my contention that the environment within which we worked did not change that much, at least not from the point of view of creativeness. Our multihued coats were soon gray with the dust of indifference and suspicion.

I don't know why I should be writing in the past tense. Isn't the theater always a concentration of the present …? Admittedly, dissidents and critics are no longer banned or jailed down there; they're only "democratically" vilified by upstarts, including government ministers who bravely hide behind parliamentary immunity—ignored, isolated, or sidelined by accusations of being "racists," "sellouts," "flunkeys of those nostalgic for lost power," "embittered egomaniacs," "revisionists unwilling to integrate the benefits of our irreversible revolution" or—horror of horrors—"liberals"!

So, little by little a new orthodoxy may well become apparent, sprouting from the same barbaric mindsets as those of the previous rulers when it comes to evaluating the bloody matter of cultural creations. We risk entering a tyranny of correctness propagating soft "values" in a newspeak I've spoken of elsewhere. A new hegemony is emerging, made up mostly of returned exiles and their obsequious and opportunistic lap-pigs manipulating the commanding posts of state and showing a growing intolerance of opposition and the asperities of criticism. The new bosses are already as rich and fat as the old ones, the only difference being that they now try and keep us on the food line in the name of "the national democratic revolution." Models may change but the machine and machinations remain the same. Power will have its way and its sway, come what may.

I don't have to remind you, my mirror shadow, of the spectacle of decaying morals and the pollution of politics around you, and that it is not only true of South Africa. I should have learned my lesson long ago and stopped thinking of any country as "my own"; I should have taken a cue from Derek Walcott who said somewhere: "My only nation is the *imagination*."

Do I need to remind you that South Africa is a construct? You know as well as I do that ideologues and political elites have been trying since the very beginning to fabricate a framework according to their visions and ideals or interests. Now, despite the changes, there seems to be constancy to the structure or the embodiment of that abstraction we call "the state"—at least, in the effects "public reality" is having on the daily lives of the people living within its frontiers.

What, you ask, are these constants (and surely not all of them are negative)?

Right you are. I thank you for the opportunity to show that I am not always darkened by doom. No, truly, I have a light heart. So let me identify a few of these "constants" for you, higgledy-piggledy: ancient and codified inequalities and injustices; seemingly irreconcilable cultural differences; diversity in beliefs and customs and lifestyles; centralized power; a conflation of state and governing party; raw capitalism diluted by conscience-allaying gestures of charity at best; good paper constitutions but weak democratic institutions; self-perpetuating racism; a history of resistance to all the above; general adherence to formal religions with scant effect on daily mores; alcoholism; gratuitous but pervasive violence both public and private; abuse of power; administrative inefficiency; a parochial patriarchy; thievery; enormous and endemic poverty; the use of dogs and rubber bullets to control people, and often sharp ammunition; a distinct civic society from quite early on; a generalized dependency on handouts; the nurturing and glorification of macho bestiality as in sport madness; a disdain for the worth of human life; worshiping "the strong leader"; political and public philistinism when it comes to the arts; hybridization; hospitality; moral schizophrenia, which is described as "adapting" to life in a harsh environment; resistance, resistance, resistance …

I said on many an occasion that we need a permanent revolution (which nobody wanted, since "normalcy" was considered the birthright we'd been deprived of for too long) in order to mediate or transform some of the extreme national traits I have just now mentioned. By that I meant that there could be no facile solutions or quick closures to our open sores and that we needed to continue building and transforming society. Our divergences and our diversity should have been considered advantages. We ought to have grasped the possibility of thinking through the *progressive* dialectical tension between shared goals and values on the one hand, and the expression of cultural multiplicities on the other. We should have known there could be no unity without a scope for the richness of particularities expressing themselves to the full.

It is a pity that we in South Africa did not understand how vitally important it is to promote free and vigorous—even conflicting—cultural spaces. I repeat: South Africa is historically, politically, and culturally a *construct*. The only way it can progress or even just find its shape is by continuing to invent it. And it is in the cultural terrain, by means of creative acts, that the *deep questions* can be identified, enunciated, shaped, and transformed: identity, memory, responsibility, hybridism, diversity, inclusive and active tolerance, the function of imagination, and the *saam-mekaar-andersmaak* (together-each-other-different-make), that is, advancing the constructive to and fro between shared national goals forged in a prolonged struggle for dignity and emancipation (maybe even "nationhood") and the specificity of mother tongue cultures and religions linked to localities and to histories (and "selfhood"). If public debate in the country continues to remain stagnant or gets stuck in the goo of power plays and excommunications, the unhealed wounds will certainly fester and our pretense at "understanding" one another will also fall apart. We will eat maggots.

Wait, wait, you may protest! Sshh, I'm getting there. I shall return to your question about the creative act and suggest that art is a source of knowledge, just as science or philosophy may be. And now I'm not speaking of museums like so many encyclopedias embalming the prevalent tastes of the rich and palming public money. Understanding, I believe, only comes in the *making*.

We (who "we"? Public authorities? Concerned citizens?) should realize that we ought to valorize hybridization while knowing full well that it does not resolve tensions and sometimes even the clashes between cultures—it just adds one more. We (again, who "we"? The artists and writers and musicians? Or those who control the means and the access to creativity?) must know that it is through artistic creativeness that the central equations of a condition such as the South African one can be approached and perhaps digested. I'm referring here, in particular, to the acceptance and the accommodation of our multiple and discrete identities, individually and collectively; to recognizing the importance of memory and working out what to do about it; to integrating the imperative of exercising responsibility for one another; to knowing that the ache for social and economic justice will not be forgotten. Because the camel is attached to its hump there is no use trying to horse it down by dressing it in a tight-fitting fur coat ...

And what I'm saying about South Africa is as true for the Americas, and increasingly also for a Europe rapidly becoming multicultured.

"We" obviously share responsibility for our story on earth and even for that invention or retrospective interpretation we so grandly call History. (The shaping of communal perception through the ordering of past times in categories and ages and aches and epochs such as the Classical Period and the Middle Ages and the Renaissance ... is always a retrospective definition.) "Collective guilt," however, is an ahistorical and apolitical enterprise. One may even suggest that it is amoral to retroactively want to impose a morality on the past in the light of present-day convictions and hypocrisies. Not only is it a self-indulgent and lazy way of simplifying intricate processes, but the accusation of group guilt (a flimsily camouflaged power play), preferably laid at the door of another tribe (and thus it soon becomes race-profiled), will also purport to paint those of us on "the right side" a paler shade of snow. "Collective guilt" promotes amnesia; it obfuscates the understanding of how and why oppressive systems and regimes come about; it obliterates the demarcations between "good" and "evil" since the criminally responsible initiators and actors can now be seen as products of group characteristics; it takes away personal responsibility; and ascribing it to the other group makes one feel so *good* about your exempted collective self. The consciousness that I will plead for on the other, slower hand implies "free will," because it leads to an understanding of the implications of our thoughts and our actions, at least potentially. As a conscious human being making my own decisions (I think), I rejected the notion of shared guilt when I *did* exercise my determination to demarcate myself from the odious tribal hegemony of the time, as did many of my tribesmen and –women each in her and his own way, and thus I'll certainly refute the need to confess to sins committed by "my people"—*if this were to be defined and confined solely by a shared color and culture* (as is the case in Fuck-land).

Besides, my friend (you are my friend, not so?), as a true believer you should know that "confession" has always been a mug's game, a shuffle of seduction between priest and sinner, interrogator and terrorist, writer and reader. The theater is not about confession, but is one then not responsible for the landscapes you evoke by walking through them?

In an addendum to the play you refer to (*Die Toneelstuk*) I recount how another close friend and comrade (not you!) wrote to query why I could not sign the collective confession of guilt and apology drawn up by some white intellectuals. One does not have to admit to *responsibility* after all, he said (he himself had been engaged in the struggle against Apartheid), but can't you at least express *regret*? Really now, didn't *all* whites benefit from that system—in education, work positions, remuneration ... just because our skin color painted us in the fortunate category?

Of course we did and of course I'm *sorry*. There's a difference, however, between putting the hand in one's own breast and beating that same breast just because one is too snooty or hypocritical to be beating the meat publicly. Recognizing the iniquitous past and trying to *understand* it in all its ambiguities and, wherever possible, within the confines of its own framework, is a necessary pageant and process of identifying why it was wrong. Indeed, I'm sorry about a hell of a lot of things. Had I been black I'd be sorry that I didn't do more to overthrow the regime of the day and thus build my self-respect on my own actions, and I'd be sorry now that so many of my kind refuse to become self-supporting and prefer to dope themselves with the pathology of victimhood. I regret the way the Hutus wiped out hundreds of thousands of Tutsis with sticks and stones. I'm sorry about the Kurds who still do not have a homeland to call their own. I'm sorry about the Palestinians oppressed by the racist and terrorist state of Israel. I regret slavery. I'm sorry about world wars and poverty and suffering and blindness and the atom bomb dropped on Hiroshima. I'm sorry about Hitler and Lenin and Mobutu and Nixon and Mugabe and Saddam. I'm starting to feel sorry for Bush. It hurts me that we just went and lost communism like a discarded childhood toy, even if it were besmirched by blood, so that we are now all flat-back camels drinking Coca-Cola. In all of this I had a part, or my people did, right from the beginning of time. They planned it all with eyes open. When my dad-and-all made me, crouched on all fours with pumping buttocks, they surely knew it was sin. I'm sorry to have been born. I regret it sincerely and promise to never ever do it again ...

Above all, I'm sorry we stopped dreaming.

So what does this help? Is creativity to be my only refuge? Am I condemned to shout an incomprehensible mumbling from the stages of exile? Of course I cannot pretend that the creative act ("the sweetest form of lying") will save my skin from contamination. Will there not always be compromises when we attempt to transform "life" into words and images? The mirror of speaking can be as obscure as the looking glass of listening. By the way, I still think it is less authoritarian to be writing the I and reading the Other than the implicit narcissism in reading the I as if it were an unchanging given and writing the Other to suit my desires.

It has been said that poetry and the practice of Zen are faced with a similar conundrum: both try to directly convey the essence of reality (or experience), knowing full well that the conveyance can only be an allusion. Or is it an illusion? Worse, the means of trying to trap reality constitutes its own realness, subject to specific laws. In poetry, as in Zen, we have reason to doubt metaphor, possibly because it so often is only an approximation. And yet, even as Zen philosophy emphasizes the inadequacy of language the practice of Zen endlessly produces "verses of truth." It attests to the fact that we just *have to* employ words (as also images and sounds) if we wish to move beyond the generic quagmire of being oinking humans. Do camels oink? The task of realism in pursuing reality beyond metaphor will always have to be accompanied by endless battles against metaphor fought through metaphors.

And even so there can be a way forward. Over the years I've had the luck on several occasions to listen to Ko-Un, an old Korean poet, reading from his work. He used to be a Zen abbot in a monastery, thus in the very center of the above tussle between the urge to transmit insights and impressions *as they are* and the approximations and autonomous reality of the diction one is obliged to use for that purpose. As far as I can see, he definitely supersedes this dichotomy. The depth of his breath would seem to make it possible for him to transform language into a direct means of presence and presentation. Indeed, his breath is a wonderful seamless cloak under which he gathers both the unsayable and words or signs as visible and audible shapes of the void. And whereas similes may be odious, metaphor as unlocking device can "marry" the very movements of language, linking convention and the beyond so that the dawning "underside" of meaning, always just at the tips of our grasp, becomes perceptible.

Am I off beam, beating about the bush for my own shadow? All of the above is interesting enough in its own right but it gets us no further, you say. We should dig deeper into the aberrations of being a clown. Do you wish me to elaborate on the ways and uses of the conception of "scapegoat"? And you think I'll be alluding to that emblem just because of recurrent attacks of acute self-pity?

Perhaps so! Although even self-pity might as well be practiced properly. In Fuck-land maybe more than elsewhere—I have to use that country as reference because that's where I got my kicks and my knocks and my knickers, and there can be no place of exile without reference to a place of origin—you yourself know how much we glorify victimhood. Blame us on history, we say. We are fashioned (buffeted, maimed, oppressed, animated) by dark forces beyond our control and understanding. We mistake the slothful ignorance of ethical implications for the pragmatic realism of closing our eyes to the unacceptable. Do we not live on a harsh continent and is it not true that Africa is not for sissies? So we embellish the cult of "the strong man"—as leader, prophet, savior, and hero, he who can give *meaning* and show the way forward. There *must* be *meaning*, damn it! And meaning, of course, will by tradition and design be simple. Indeed, we believe we are entitled to simple and meaningful "truths."

The dissident, he/she who brings doubt into the house like a stinking rat, must be ignored, ridiculed, or chased away.

The effect of this macho mumbo-jumbo is a brutalization of public awareness, a dumbing down of shared intelligence, a reinforcement of our traditional patriarchal and hierarchical social structures, a confirmation of religious orthodoxies and political barbarism and cultural hegemonies, a renunciation of personal responsibility, an impediment to the development of vigorous civil societies, a repression of the creative power of creolization, a flourishing of hypocrisy—and a spewing out of the doubter.

The other intimate side of the scapegoat identity, if you turn over the coin, is that he or she will be an "icon." Fascinating, by the way, how words screw one another, how a meaning will change with the shift of a letter. If you take the *f* out of *shiftage*—in Amharic a *shifta* is a bandit—it just becomes excretion. The prophet, when he stumbles, will be sacrificed in expiation of society's anguish; the priest will become a gangster. The need to focus hope on an individual remains. And so the athlete or the singer, Maradona and Madonna, will be expected to fulfil the daddy function of *leading* by providing *meaning*. It is absurd!

As for me, I'm neither prophet nor priest and not even a soccer player of note—just the fool walking my shadow on the stage of an empty theater.

OK, enough of that. I'm sure you must be nearly as sorry for me as I am for myself, but it is of scant interest. Let us rather one last time unroll the ball of twine to where we started from because, despite your protestations, it is not possible to cut the line conclusively. How would I comment on the boundedness of identities on the one hand (for example, the broad sense of belonging to a group of people who share the same language, the same history, and the same place) and, on the other, the evolving yet perfectly complete self-in-metamorphosis evoked in the work, which can be symbolized, probably correctly, as some form of theater in exile—I mean, as in making a spectacle of myself?

I understand this latter self, this "I" in the poem or painting, which is premised on transformation, to always be reinventing its self (if *it* can have a *self*) as a matter of principle. In this direction lies the potential for renewal and change, for relating to the familiar in new and creative ways. But is it possible to marry this state of being to a sense of belonging and of social community, so often ring-fenced by specific traditions or limiting ways of thinking? In short, is it possible to keep changing without getting lost?

The "identity" we speak of here is the result of a process of awareness. Also, of distancing. "It" comes into being through consciousness. "To study the self is to forget the self," Zen master Dogen said. (He might also have said: "To study the self is to find a *you*.") In meditation you can watch the mind or consciousness at work, you may turn it over to look at the maggots squirming and the ants hiding from the sun. One could parody Descartes by positing: "'It' (consciousness) thinks, therefore an 'I' is thought."

I don't believe the existence or the sense of "self" predates the process, even though there are aspects of identity—inherited cultural traits—which you or I have or may have been given as inherence without knowing so, and these we may uncover only later in life. Like growing humps. There may well be a blueprint. But the aging body thinks differently; the shadow gets stooped. In other words, what I call "identity" is the reflection of a process to which all our senses and attributes, such as memory and imagination, contribute. (In Buddhism this "bundle" making up the "self" consists of *skandhas*.)

If you know this you can trace how the various components of "self" interact to generate consciousness. The moment there is consciousness there is inevitably a "self" as clearinghouse or as ghost host. The trick is to move from house to house following the wind without becoming attached to slammed doors. That is why I say *the I is a mirror to the self*. Or the other way around: *the self is mirror to the I*. The apparent difficulty would seem to be how to crest "the moment of taking note," using a (temporarily) fixed take on the self to serve as orientation and situation from where to recognize the "process" which is change and motion. (That too, is why I claim *thing is process*, i.e., our appreciation of its "thing-ness" is never static, quite beside the fact that the object—and the subject!—will be going through modifications however slow, due to aging and stooping and positioning as defined by the wind.) Mind is the wind to which the camel lifts its snout to neigh in utter longing.

To be sure, this sense of I (identity, the I-ing of self, the dent made by the eyeing, id-entity, I-density) is dependent on interaction with some non-I or some body "out there." Community is usually the mirror and the stage is the shadow-land where I and Other meet. "I am a human through people." We identify/situate ourselves in our interaction with and relation to cultural constructs such as language, religion, ideology, a shared narrative of history or destiny, our adherence or resistance to specific values. Ultimately, we may be exiled to the stage to realize that we are all naked rats sniffing for poison, but we would have seen the play from the wings in the meantime. The shaping of the recognition of identity and the resultant (self) identification is very much the product of a given society and of a trajectory of circumstances.

For the border prowler involved in the transformation and expansion of awareness it is *consciousness* that matters, the flow with its rhythms and breaks—not the successive stops and crutches and crotch-snatches of I. "I" is but the focal (fecal?) and transit point, and transition, of perception. *"Movement* is the *thing."* The awareness of awareness grows from the constant dialectical movement between self and non-self. (One could say: I have met God; he/she/it begins where I stop. You could also say: I am not the nation.) Self is mirrored in non-self, and the other way around. Self is ever-expanding emptiness—which doesn't mean it isn't cluttered and clamorous with voices; more precisely, the *awareness* of the changing, making, and unmaking of "self" is the dilation of emptiness. There is no "self," only "selving." One is always becoming nothing. Put differently, one is always becoming death. And that's as physical a fact as a black cat!

No awareness of perception except through I; growing perception brings the rubbing out of I. This is what is known as: *using the I to destroy it.*

From what I've tried to say now flow a number of observations referring to your questions, my dear Reader. Mirror, in a manner of speaking, is the tool and the manifestation of self. This is self-evident! Mirror is "soul." Mirror is the other without whom or which there can be no looking back. Ego, dying in the glass as it is smothered with earth is the departing echo of being; it is the memory of glass. Measuring the time of remembering will allow you to establish the distance between the small bang of inception when the glass implodes, and the bleeding fetus of definition. One is never just one fixed identity—except maybe in the arbitrariness of some administrative grid. One always consists of many selves, shoals, and shelves and elves of self, depending on the need or the circumstances and environment—private/public, child/woman/mother/lover, Afrikaner/South African/human/exile/uncitizen … What we know as memory may well be the dwelling-place, the dumping ground, of all these salvaged ghostly selves, the "ancestors," the "ghosts of saved and unsaved versions of history competing for attention."

To "itself" self is a compass, not a map. Sometimes it is a grace of forgetting. To society self is a way of being and of behaving. Descartes, it would seem, had as a motto "Larvatus prodeo" (I set out behind an actor's mask). This allows for an interesting link between the larva waiting to become the butterfly of death, and mask! As well, that I move for and toward "God"!

Martin Versveld, our old master philosopher (you'll certainly agree, he was such a vigorous walker!) wrote: "The ego is the mask of the person." In this sense then identity is a mask imagined by communal traditions, conventions, and expectations: a larva in the process of becoming the moth that will fly away like angel shadow.

Thirteen

SELF-PORTRAIT/DEATHWATCH

A Note on Autobiotrophy

I/Other. I don't find it pleasant to be turning over the leaves of my-self, and yet I'm doing so all the time. When I describe an onion on the tablecloth I am detailing the self. God did not make this world: I did—conceiving the vibrant thoughts, the rolling hills, the scattering shadows, the holes in the ground, the ants, including God. How do you know my thoughts are not hills? More, I am still creating the world and I may stop at any moment.

Why is it unpleasant then? Because consciousness is open-ended and subject to constant change and it is frightening if not perilous to keep on caressing the unknowable I. The hidden nature of awareness is that it cannot be stilled for long enough to be defined, not even tem-porarily like the dead person. If I do thus write about some id or other oddment it must be dead. Therefore I cannot write *about* me; I could only *write I.* And immediately the writing is blanched, staunched. Be-comes *it.* The fly in amber. God in his grave. Even though there is no gravy the ants will not go hungry. Writing as weak awareness, a minute manifestation of movement stilling death.

It would be more illuminating to trace the trajectories of Panus, Elephterià, King Fool, Don Espejuelo, Geta Wof, Jan Blom, Vagina Jones, Lazarus, Comrade Ekx, Afrika Aap, or Bangai Bird ... To get *you* at the tip of my pen or into the word processor: I the Other or/ and the other Other. Or to be free to create the third persons. It would indeed have been more than satisfying to paraphrase the true immortal self as Pier Paolo Pasolini, as Frantz Fanon, as Bertolt Brecht, as Billy Bodyday, as Matrice Mulumba, as Gueux Guevara, as Pablo Picasso, as Ho-Ho Hinh, as Manet Magritte, as G. Goya, as Fou Fu ... But the commission is to briefly sketch the public one, the orator, the poet in flux and in flop. Also, I assume, to point in passing at those of us—all but one—who fell dead by the roadside or gloriously died on the bridge—which translates as this and that about the past. And in such a way to create history. History is the mother of invention. It protrudes and it is concave. It is open-minded. It is stained by the dead weight of what you have lived through, but it also delineates the absence of what you did not experience. I shall write about this "you" in order to duck the blame, to shift the weight, to sculpt the breathing space. Perhaps to blame the duck. The mathematically Immaculate Conception, then, of the mask known as Breyten Breytenbach.

◆

Young/Old. In the beginning there is the verb. (Then the verbrhoea.) I was born many years ago in a small town called Bonnievale in the southwestern region of a state then still known as the Union of South Africa. (In 1961 it became the Republic of South Africa and still later, after a prolonged race war that pitted the least contaminated sectors of the Third World against the Western democracies, it was to become the People's Republic of Azania.) My parents were of poor peasant stock. I had a twin brother, who died at birth, and three more brothers and a sister. My mother passed away and was buried in the hills above the sea when I was doing my apprenticeship to freedom as a political prisoner; if you were to cock an ear you might yet hear her chuckling there. My father is alive and well and living in South Africa, even though he stopped talking four years ago.

As in other "new" countries with like stories of conquest and colonialism, South Africans too would move from town to town and from job to job in an attempt to escape the taste of failure. In a similar pattern my people navigated over the face of the Boland—the "Upper Country," a radius of 200 kilometers from the Cape of Good Hope, the ancient grazing grounds of the now extinct Khoi people—and the bordering areas. It is without the tiniest bird of doubt the most beautiful land in the world. In the back of my mind there is even now the green motions of the two oceans.

When I was young I was intelligent. I went to school and subsequently to the University of Cape Town to study Fine Arts and Letters. I had already started painting and writing poetry to express my infatuation with loss and my exquisite sensibility. There were many flying foxes in the fruit trees. I would gradually learn and unlearn the adjectives. Then I dropped out of university to become a drifter—a creator, I fondly thought. I was on my way to sartori. Little did I know it was also the jump into free fall away from the strictures of my tribe—which would yet leave me with the scar tissue of structures. I was going into the wide world, entering the many homes of exile, ultimately to be purged by poverty and prison and to become familiar with the poetry of politics.

Now I am old and stupid and facing a Chinese landscape shifting into focus and then forgetting itself: like a dream fading into memory, a thought washed away in shades of pale ink. Rather be verb than verbal, I say to my autobiographer. (Or verbose.)

◆

Black/White. Calvinists hold to the dogma of predestination. Essentially it means coming to terms with being part of God's embroidery. It means, I think, accepting the salutary relief of fatalism. It also implies assuming there is an *order* to life, to all that quiver and copulate in the celestial spheres and down hither—even down into the past or into the murky subconscious, which, of course, is the passage to India discovered by Christopher Freud. This order has its temporal translation. Our terrestrial masters have the God-given *right* to rule and the interests of the State are paramount. (The State is God incarnate among men.) Many roads lead to totalitarianism, the power malady, but the above conception constitutes, I dare believe, a shortcut to the priorities of law and security, to the inviolability of property, to the entrenched privileges of the strong, to holy wars, capital punishment, whiteness, and charity.

◆

Threaded through the Oriental approach to life is the belief in karma—or the legacies of that teaching, or the vital positioning vis-à-vis and interaction with the past and present histories of people holding to that belief. Hinduism and Buddhism also have their bodies of laws and custom—given half a finger the pious acolytes will go on droning forever to embroider the obscurantist mind, their chants becoming clear like rancid butter—but karma at least confers personal responsibility and it allows for the breaking of the wheel, the waking from the coma of cause and effect. The Way makes the Law irrelevant.

I was born in a state where the white/black order was immutable. It warped all of us because even when we revolted against the tyranny of Apartheid—the maiming of the social body and the corruption of the private mind—it was a shadow play in order to have an orthodoxy replaced by another ... I was born *white* (we are now talking of bureaucratic arbitration, tribal superstitions, and ideological genetics, not nature), immediately a member of the master race, growing up under the signs of chlorosis. But as I started backing into the inner reaches of expanding consciousness I realized that my heart was *black*. You could say my heart is a nightclub for the printer's devil. And it is the abjuration of the denial of my humanity, this unending trip toward integration that I try to trace by the leucorrhoea, the *fluor albus* of my writing.

And I am convinced that life, and the definitions by which we attempt to immobilize it (understanding is death), is an infinite and goalless process of metamorphosis—posited though, I should bloody well hope, on the meticulous search for jumps and breaks. The lion's roar explodes the jackal's mind. In terms of social arrangements the "jump" would be a revolution, a breakthrough to the suspension or the obliteration of pairs and opposites.

I may still be bird or horse or stone. It is also not a bad idea from time to time to open the manhole and pass down some embroidery or acupuncture needles to God; it is damp in the warrens of the subconscious, one risks contracting rheumatism of the articulations there, rigidity of the limbs, and repeated movements may do no more than just grease the joints. Perhaps I should not forget the pen and paper.

◆

African/European. I realize that my expectations, my apprehensions, my instinctive recognition of *the right position and place* (read for this, if you wish, the unquestioned sense of security, of belonging), the means by which I experience space and rhythm and structure or the way of my relationship to the environment and to other people, my notion of breath and/or breathing space that flows from mountains and a cloud very high in the sea-colored sky, that which reverberates as "blue" in me if you were to utter the signifier, as in *blue like a coffin*—that this substratum that constitutes the self-memory of my being was formed during the tender prerational years in Africa. I am an African.

There is in me the bedrock that can never be non-African. And then I was to become European too. I first arrived in Lisbon after traveling fourth class in a swinging hammock down the hold of a liner that dropped anchor in all the Portuguese African ports. Black stevedores were at that time still driven along with whips. They weren't really black; their skin had a sickly gray pallor. Off the Cape Verde islands we shipped more voyagers who squatted in the bows the whole day long, singing wistful songs and staring at the emerald waves to see the sun plumb the depths. I was twenty years old with pipe and beard and rucksack and twenty British pounds in my pocket. It was the European winter of 1960.

Then, in South Africa, there bloomed the massive campaigns of resistance to Apartheid, led by the Pan-Africanist Congress (PAC) and the African National Congress (ANC)—culminating in a chain of bloody repression with the Sharpeville massacre as its apotheosis. The black nationalist formations were banned, so too the South African

Communist Party. People went into exile or entered the prisons. Doors clanged shut. Nelson Mandela set out on his long walk to freedom, his dead life, his martyrdom. Abroad I got to know and sympathize and start collaborating with my militant compatriots, patriots all.

I had been to Spain where I made the acquaintance of Mr. Goya with the silvery pants and the rosy buttocks and the black bowels. The Guardia Civil still wore patent leather hats as if acting out some Lorca poem, and they stank of death. In the Jura I got singingly pissed on home-brewed liqueurs and in London on dark beer. I worked on farms and stations and in factories just long enough to qualify for the dole; I taught English in Bergen, which was buried under snow and darkness, and earned one plate of food a day as a portraitist in a nightclub in Nice. Sidney Bechet's "La Petite Fleur" was the jukebox hit. I signed up on a yacht in the Mediterranean and took part in a mutiny in the port of St. Ives. I slept under bridges and on vacant lots and near Hamburg in some rustling orchard and on the road to Newcastle curled up in the snow on the back of a "donkey" used for heating an adjacent greenhouse. There was a white cat and I thought it must be the soul of my mother trying to mew to me in Afrikaans. I thought she must have died, but she continued writing to me via the American Express. I celebrated my twenty-first birthday in the Kasbah of Tangier, wrapped in a brown camelhair burnoose with my arm around the neck of a beast of burden. With fellow bums and runaways I'd take my turn to warm a gray-sheeted single bed in some sleazy hotel room. And in an ancient sector of Paris I met Lady Lotus. We ran off to be married and for many years survived on the income from her salary. Vietnamese cooking became my favorite nourishment.

In 1964 I started publishing in Afrikaans. Poetry and prose. Robert Rimbaud had disdainfully turned down abject pleas to become my

mentor. I'd continue publishing Afrikaans works right through the sixties and the early seventies, then take a break and start again in 1983.
Extracts would later be translated into several tongues and eventually I
was to begin doing my thing in English and in French. When in Rome
you do as the Christians do. You become invisible. I painted in small
rented garrets or in other people's studios and exhibited the results.
Some paintings were taken off the walls or had to be blocked out because of obscenity.

Those were the radical sixties. In South Africa a generation of
black writing was wiped out by censorship, banishment, incarceration,
booze and suicide; a generation of white writing won the freedom to
be sodomized by the tribal authorities, some of them ministers of the
church, and the grunting authors turned to Europe for intellectual
sophistry and decadence as ostensible sustenance—in reality a face-sav-
ing device, even though it may be incongruous to save face when on all
fours. In Paris I moved with Black Panther hijackers, revolutionary
Brazilians, Kurds, Greeks, freedom fighters from Mozambique and
Angola ... I frequented a few of the charismatic leaders who lived in
the shadowy passages of history. There would be assassinations, as of
my handler Henri Curiel by French counter-intelligence agents carrying out a joint Israeli-South African contract ... "We" lost Chile and,
for a while, Argentina and Greece; but "we" won Vietnam, Laos, Por-
tugal, Mozambique, Angola, Zimbabwe, and Guinea Bissau. "They"
killed Lumumba, Luthuli, Ben Barka, Martin Luther King, Mond-
lane, Guevara, Malcolm X, Amilcar Cabral ... The Russians nipped
in the bud the Prague spring. The permanent nature of imperialist
appetites became abundantly clear. Africa grew poorer. Gradually the
preeminence of the late twentieth-century empire's capital, New York,
emerged and it was soon obvious we'd have to face and counteract all

kinds of carnivorous cultural stratagems. Bourgeois leftists to their horror suddenly discovered the Gulag and the totalitarian nature of most communist parties and promptly moved to the right of the political spectrum, shat their bitter narcissism all over Third Worldism and forsook philosophy for fiction. Central European existential anguish was to become the locus of politically engaged intellectualism, democracy was decreed to be an exclusively European virtue, capitalism became a moral imperative, French intellectuals were ubiquitous as television donkeys braying for the blood of the infidels. Africa grew poorer ... But all that came later. First there was the *baroud d'honneur* of May 1968 ...

Europe made me a world citizen, but it also caused me to become more aware of my Africanness. Inevitably there would be returns to "the dark continent." For some time I even held a genuine Algerian passport. I came to identify more and more with the complex wars of the Third World against disfiguration, for dignified survival, for true autonomy, for alternative economic circuits. I realized that the privileged role ascribed to the Judeo-Christian heritage when talking about "civilization" was nothing but the prejudiced and partisan and faulty interpretation of later manipulators; that "Western values"—the cloak of expansionism—occulted alternative sources: Chinese, Arab, African ... I saw that the definition of "progress" was tendentious and that applying it meant opting for a terrible crunching power mechanism. I could not picture myself as a *white man*, not even in bastardized shape. I am an African bastard—from a world where *métissage* is continually absorbed; Africa, the continent where the reality of metamorphosis is paramount, where you have the chance of seeing the simplest object transformed into a votive symbol or a still point of magic; where there is a humbleness traversed by flashes of extravagant glory like flowers suddenly bursting upon an arid landscape, and the innate knack of living on the zero horizon of survival; where people don't have either/or minds but nonetheless master dialectics effortlessly to make of it a joyful game of trictrac; where bourgeois values are nearly totally absent, or at least those power relationships based on possessions or exploitation, or at least that materialism linked to the profit motive only which would incarnate—as in the West—a pathological need to dominate and to recover lost and innocent certainties; a continent allowing for *other* readings of art, its functions and those of the artist (often hereditary), for humor; where there is still such a legacy of humanism that Africa even now cannot truly work up the necessary revulsion to spit out the abject South African whites. Africa, where the whores are not outcasts, but may and do become scented government ministers. Africa, as I said, where your worth is not painted by what you have—though a watch plated with gold and a ghetto blaster would be things of awe and mirth—but by how you are, by what you do to and for others.

◆

Interior/Exile. I have consistently rejected the concept of exile as debilitating, petrifying, self-pitying—and yet again, many of my ruminations have circled around the condition of absence: not being where I belong naturally. I have tried to show up the negative aspects and the positive acquisitions of being expelled from the tribal framework and then permanently living *elsewhere*. It is true that you not only live outside the social and physical pattern where you could have functioned instinctively and completely, but that you must also accommodate the lack, the absence, the feeling of having been deprived of normal expectations. There is some alienation involved here, a land-sickness, a han-

kering after booming breakers and the mordant wit of a drunken proletariat and ripe stars and the weighty perfume of gardenias embalming
the night on a darkened veranda. But elsewhere you survive, as if in
compensation, with an accrued knack for adaptation; you get to inspect
the inner lining of "integration"; you are given distance as a consolation
prize and perhaps you gain perspective too; at last you experience the
self as God hiding in the burrow of his grave, with the febrile dance
steps and movements of meaning of the ant.

When I left the native shores in early 1960 I had no intention of
heroically going into the suffering of exile. In fact, I gradually graduated
into absence without ever being able to solve the ambiguities of my state
of suspension. Like other lame-winged locusts, I also became an early
morning habitué of the Prefecture de Paris, hoping to renew my *carte de
sejour*. It was only in 1973 that I was allowed to return "home" for three
months and then, as reported in *A Season in Paradise*, the trip turned out
to be an effort to come to terms with my roots, to be finished with the
business of youth. Unsuccessfully so, as soon became evident—or else
I'm but a vulgar recidivist—because my clandestine return during 1975
was also partly motivated by the private need to go beyond the contradiction of being passionately involved with "down there" while living
happily abroad. Finally, after seven and a half years of lying at a loose
end in prison like a pulse beat in the heart of No Man's Land, having
attachment leached from me, that umbilical cord was cut. Thereafter I
could continue, knowing that South Africa would always be the private
mother-prism and pain, as well as a luck, and a daunting challenge to all
of humanity to lift our dull eyes to a new horizon during this last dash
of the century. I was liberated to fully live my leftover life elsewhere. To
move with the changes. To paint and to write. To see sky come shrink-
ing closer. To take in Brother Death as nosy boarder.

This "non-involvement" is not at all to the liking of the maggots that live on the morally revolted body of anti-Apartheid the same way others—cigar-chomping vultures and stripe-suited hyenas—continue feasting off the beastliness itself. It is of no use saying I am not an exile: people would insist on having their need for outrage and public evisceration and catharsis satisfied.

The diaspora of South Africans probably reinforced an important component of our struggle: internationalism—eventually also in the beneficial sense of Pan-Africanism and of Third World consciousness, and not only as socialist prattle—thereby saving the process from being just another nationalist black uprising.

◆

Free/Unfree. I am a statutory, convicted terrorist. This I am inordinately proud of although I realize how easy it is to become one in the perverted context of South Africa—where, after all, we encounter a population of five million albinos and twenty-five million actual or would-be terrorists. Our exclusiveness has been vulgarized, our mythological nature ridiculed! We are becoming as common as garden tourists!

I have covered many pages with reflections and speculations pertaining to freedom, as if obliterating my tracks. Perhaps not enough, as time has whitened the words into the unsaid. The snow is like a sleeve of silence. Still, I have come up with quotable thoughts even if these were filched from other minds. Should one not be free to steal?

This concern with freedom evidently became more acute after my conviction in November 1975 for underground activities detrimental to the security of the state of South Africa. In fact, I was digging holes for the white rulers. The subsequent prison years constituted a laboratory experience of the mechanics of freedom.

Then, early in December 1982, came release—and captivity. Not only because I had become conditioned to tail wagging, not simply because the mind was now sly like a hunted, lascivious beast, but because I was henceforth to be made a convict of respectability and accountability. I have seen. I am responsible. I must report. And so my own books hemmed me in; all these images like specters took possession of my eyes to deform my vision. And here I am now, writing myself, burrowing into an inextricable labyrinth!

We should, Tagore said, be entitled to the right to freedom, the right to nature, the right to remember. I add: the right to forget, to be cowardly, to the fuckup as creative vector. How could there be insight without a break in vision? The pressure to conform, from friend and from foe, is enormous and permanent; we all live and participate in the conspiracy of mediocrity; we are all sucked into the need to make believe that life is worth living since it generates sense—and not so much "life" as each one of our individual miserable existences. One has then to fight for the freedom to be a failure, a heretic.

◆

The debate would, however, benefit from being centered rather on the intimate interaction between freedom and effectiveness in the field of keeping the options open. It is not necessarily shameful to be living at the table of the political lord or that of the patron of the arts, be it as fool or entertainer. The wine is often good there. Nor is it intrinsically wrong to be a kept woman or a gigolo. But one should do so as the chameleon; one must not only be a master of disguises, patiently stalking the fly and rotating the eyes in different directions simultaneously, but willing, furthermore, to act as the transformer of situations and relationships. In Africa the chameleon (or "walk-softly") is the agent of transformation, the bearer of tidings that there will always be life, from one digestion to the next, and thus immortal-ity—but it must be noted that he can also be used as the main ingre-dient of a very potent poison. And remember the words of Ka'afir, the poet: "At birth the chameleon is transparent."

True, you will be defined in your continuing attempts to define the inchoate. I think Baudelaire called it "correspondences."

◆

Clarity/Consciousness. By now it should be abundantly clear that I am digging for ways to keep on undermining the perimeters, the boundaries of clarity, the "established law and order." More than death I fear the living mummification of understanding and meek acceptance (it *is* a death-life); the arbitrariness, the petrifaction resulting from felicitous expression and lucid definition. When somebody says to you, "I know," put a stone under his tongue and slit his throat and read the red stone for gurgitated *meaning.* When the weak-hipped intellectual advances whiskey in hand to claim, "We are the avant-garde," offer him/her a wheelchair and a *Playboy* to masturbate over.

Si Dios vive, todo esta permitido. But the quest for freedom, acting as if you were free, imposes upon you the bind of having to make decisions *all* the time, from naught to nuclear. It is very tiring, alienating. (What is *iz,* what was *waz.*) The civic poet owes it to the community to be a thorn in the flesh, but also to his fellow travelers to keep on tripping

himself up—for the sake or the chance of integrity that is not an attri-
bute but a method, a tool for scraping the crap from his perceptions.

Consciousness is a question of leaps and bounds and crack-ups,
and painful reappraisals. And then the slow knitting of the torn flesh.
It is the flame licking and spitting at the wick of the spine. It is the
flowing stream with "sense" an occasional surface-flash that makes you
think it may be stilled into a mirror. Consciousness makes no sense
except that it may lose a syllable or two to become conscience.

I remember getting up at night in my cell, which was like a hole,
to do *zazen* facing the dark concrete mirror of the wall. And a moon
of nothingness would rise. I also remember Moucho Marx saying: "I
started from nothing to end with nothing, but all by myself."

One thing is not more beautiful or more useful or more spiritual
than the other. There can be no hierarchy of aesthetics. For me the
practice of beauty shapes the private parts of ethics. ("History protrudes and is concave.") Neither can there be withdrawal from political
or ethical commitment; there is no irreconcilable contradiction between creation and engagement—rather, they are as two tensions of
the same striving. Aesthetics flow into ethics, which leads to action.
An act of beauty is a political statement.

◆

Responsible/Subversive. For there remains the anger at what we are
doing to ourselves, the hunger for silence, the rage to create, the need
to transform (and be transformed). No guilt: *That* we have as legacy
from the Old Man in the burrow, and only in action can it be dis-
solved. In any event, we need it like we need a hole in the head.

◆

I believe we are much more alert to our surroundings than we can afford to admit. I also believe that we transmit far more sensitivity than we wish to know—by allusion, the nonverbal meanings of our rhythms and our sounds, especially by our hesitations and our stumbling, the structural gaps and silences in our language. By the unsaid, in a manner of speaking. Which is another illustration of how the Law is a husk: made up of the *meaning*—worse, the *interpretation* of words.

Part of the civic poet's responsibility is to recognize the interstices, to be the thin wedge that could split the cracks, to seize the distaff elements and the moments of disequilibria. He must be able to exploit the dynamic dialectical relationship of illusion, or appearance, with reality—knowing intimately the myriad ways in which the one becomes the other. The poet must be subversive. By word and by deed and by word-deed he continues to detonate the responsible certainties—in an ongoing attempt to break into the apparent/void.

Frantz Fanon cried out: "Oh, my body, make of me a man who will always be asking questions." He also said: "I don't want to chant the past at the expense of now and of the future. I only insist on one thing: that the enslavement of man by man—that is of me by another—should cease forever. May I be allowed to discover and to want man wherever he may be found." And: "The colonized 'thing' becomes human through the very process by which he frees himself."

The foregoing is concretized in a critical relationship to the Left (or what's left of it)—where it means to subscribe to and participate in the struggle for generosity and tolerance and international solidarity with those deprived of their freedom and their human rights; when it means the willingness to keep working for greater democracy and better justice and more power to the people; where freedom is defined as a continuous battle, and one is made to think oneself into being and to comprehend the origins and the mechanisms of social organisms; where elitism is refused and the bringing about of some new orthodoxy, some school of cultural terrorism and atrophy, another power monopoly—be it hypocritically claimed in the name of the tongueless proletariat—are rejected for ever. And then to translate all of the above into praxis.

◆

To Be/Or Not to Be. Is indeed not the question. Even in your "no longer being" you should be a disruptive force. Death is an exile, a perch from which to jump further. You could die ridiculously, beaten to death in some sad wasteland between Rome and Ostia, or by slicing your innards open on a clean mat. Or you could continue living, feeding your slow suicide on metaphor and color ...

I slip from dream to waking and back again, from homage to derision, from emptiness to love. Books to write and pictures to paint and political consciousness to be broken open. To be an eye to the landscape—and be part of it? To be. Not to be. And to be.

◆

Go on/Go on. I remember writing the above in July 1986 at Can Ocells, probably sitting at the rough worktable outside on the patio and being intoxicated by the smell of jasmine. I conceived of the piece as a gesture honoring the memory of Pier Paolo Pasolini, although I had never met him. It was a moment of taking stock but also of trying to empty the mind of the clutter of accumulated life. Death-in-life is when one had become too full of thoughts and opinions and memories.

I remember looking out over the distant Pyrenees, hazy in the summer air of Catalonia, and anticipating the glint of snow that would cover the ridges in winter and make everything sharp and clear. I had covered many pages with reflections and speculations pertaining to freedom, as if obliterating my tracks in the search for a road. Perhaps not enough; time whitened the words into the unsaid. The snow I longed for would be a sleeve of silence.

The prison was fading. Exactly a year later we would bring together in Dakar, Senegal, and then on to Ouagadougou and to Accra, the first major meeting between the ANC, still in exile, and about sixty community leaders from inside South Africa. By then I was again working with a network of friends and accomplices, which made the breakthrough possible. A consequence of this series of historical encounters that would facilitate the negotiations for a peaceful transition toward majority rule of the troubled country was the establishment of the Gorée Institute on the old slave island off the coast of Dakar. This Pan-African institution with its roots in African civil societies was dedicated, as a center of excellence, to promoting processes of democratization and development and culture in Africa.

I didn't know it yet, but when "freedom" finally came to South Africa, beyond the release of Nelson Mandela and the establishment of a new constitution in the early '90s, I would find that there was for me no way back. I would have friends and accomplices, but no more comrades. All over the continent, political elites were beginning to eviscerate our dreams of liberation and of progress. Sometime I would return to the land of my birth, the breakers would boom on beaches where early in the morning one could still see the fresh tracks of shy buck, and the proletariat was drunk as ever on moon and on mountain air—but I was now a stranger there. I had finally arrived in the Middle World.

Time would pass. Books would be written and paintings painted. I found that when I attempted to describe an onion on the tablecloth I was in reality detailing layers of the self or that which for lack of a better concept, and out of laziness, could be called a "self." There would be no god to make the world we lived in, even in retrospect, because we came from nowhere, and we humans were besmirching it with the encroaching shadows of an eternal night. But it was still possible— indeed, necessary—to conceive of vibrant thoughts, of rolling hills, the scattering shadows and the holes in the ground, the ants, including an imagined God. How could I ever know my thoughts were not hills? More, I was still creating the world and my hands were about to abandon me at any moment.

Was it unpleasant? I'm slowly getting to the point where I will not remember. But it could not have been all bad. There was no longer an "unknowable I" to be caressed. Consciousness is open-ended and subject to constant change and it is frightening. I could only *write I*, that changing entity stiffening in death while taking on the glistening eternity of snow. By continuing to live in order to feed the slow suicide on metaphor and color …

Fourteen

FOR MICHAEL FRIED

Paris, December 21, 2004

we live in dark times
birds of heaven are poisoned
we roam through brightly lit halls
stare myopically at exhibitions
of gray imaginaries, encyclopedias of passing
meticulously annotated absences of sense

the emptier the contents the more painful
perfection and the perfidy of looking will flow
as the world completes itself through us
and we see corpse camps, genocide, man
abjuring his skein of belonging
in a desperate wing-beat to be
free of death
the birds of heaven are poisoned
and we live in dark times

and somewhere on fetid waters of holy rivers
burning effigies of dark-faced goddesses bob
they've long since stopped singing to us
in closet spaces we stare myopically
at the skinned life of the writer

naked like a soft dragon on the floor
to kiss a black tongue to the shoe
of his cruel beloved
the spine a curve of cursed words
and we see death camps, genocide, troughs
stuffed with corpses, man
jeering at his rope of legitimacy
in a thrashing wing-thrust
to be free of passing,
has long since stopped singing to us

"finally, when I shave my somber morning face
I have the impression of shaving
my cadaver before it is put on its bier
and let to water
in the putrid river of oblivion"

from the void comes incarnation
comes dark wind
will the wind be a wound
and signal the blind child

in twilit cellar chambers
we eat salad and lard and bread
suddenly recall the stories of illicit ancestors
how clumsily our mouths fold around deceased tongues
to elicit murmurs of forgetting
man relinquishes the illumination
of ever again being mad and clear

and out there the clear city rises
magnificent ruin of man's monstrous imagination
where much love was committed
and murders often done by knife
while the writer sang

of incandescent rivers where goddesses bathe
the water dragon naked and blind

to the left a high moon slips
as petrified subconsciousness
chafed pale by dust of space and time

tomorrow paper snow will litter and letter
the roof-map and the nest of streets
and from gutters icy drops will drip
on dark faces of shivering wanderers

Fifteen

TO BRING TO BOOK

We live in dark times.

Can one "own" a painting? Or a book? What one has is a moment of having and if you're lucky, if the work reveals enough texture to engage consciousness and sufficient structure to allow its own sense to be released, it will be a mirror on time and thus it will come into being as "captured" movement. Time will come to pass in you.

Objects crafted around the stillness of movement encapsulate the potential for change, of becoming other and making other, producing perhaps unintended meanings. Naturally, such a process opens the way to alienation (time is the mother element of displacement), to one's losing possession and control so that the very self becomes a kaleidoscope, and to the paradoxical satisfaction of being able to say: "I do not own myself; I've given myself away." (But, "What you cannot give away you will lose.") I hoped to set off here a procedure that would *alter* and not just lay wilted words on the *altars* of the generally agreed upon.

The fragments making up this "book," were written and sometimes rewritten over the most recent years—except for "Self-portrait/Death-watch," first published in slightly different form as an essay to go with a volume of prison poems called *Judas Eye*. The notes were repeatedly (you may say redundantly) informed by the notion of a Middle World, a space of becoming that cannot partake of the certainties of leaving or the satisfaction of arrival and is all the better for it. For a long time the working title, as I tried to echo the steps of retrieval, was *MOR,* the place stretching from love to death. At a later stage, I decided to call the coalescing collection, *On the Noble Art of Walking in No Man's Land.*

(*"Since I've been sentenced and brought to this Death Row, I even started drafting a memoir. I thought to call it* On the Noble Art of Walking in No Man's Land. *It is fragmentary, and as I advance it becomes clear that it is a possible description of the undertow of a given surface, a piling up of images like the breakup of an ice floe. The ice of experiences and impressions becomes a slough of water. In due time this will evaporate to become a cloud in the heavens, rain, rivulets, stream, sea—to be frozen over with winter. Death, to survive, must be deep-frozen."—A. Niemand, in* Memory of Snow and of Dust.)

The pieces are shifting reflections illustrating emergent templates or territories of (the) self and this world—as it were swimming around in the imagined "I," floundering really, until such time as one felt something to stand on, even if only the slippery shell of the primal tortoise on whose back all creation is posited. Another way of explaining would be that one (which one?) was accompanying the inward unfolding of identity toward that nothingness that cannot be reduced. Some stories engaged with the shift of power we are subjected to in the world where fundamentalisms are threatening to push us over the abyss; others again returned (again and again) to Africa or walked around "the things we do in exile." The greatest danger is always the loss of diversity, even as our footprints are the same. That is why we need to dress up memory in distinctive garments with embroidered hems.

Writing ought to be able to draw from the virtual or the potential a concretization that cannot be undone, and thereby permit a "sense of things." Rhythm elicits music. Heavy black anger when pushed far enough becomes light—witness the fun of a Beckett or a Burroughs—and then the writer can dance with the reader. Imagination does not exist until you have performed it. I wished to bow low, sweep a hand, and invite you to this dancing on paper. See the wind fluttering the garments. Was it because you were strange, a foreigner, that we might know one another, that I could dream to be like you? And you like me?

A snippet of some Mahayana Buddhist text reads: "Difference is identity; identity is difference."

In any event, one was trying to use knowledge as a vector for awareness; one also "knew" that consciousness generates and constitutes a knowing of its own account.

Knowledge is usually verifiable and awareness ought to be demonstrable, but both will be *altered* by the dialectic of interaction. God has a double: it is his imagination. And whatever we do not understand is free. Listen, when nothing is left the music throbs with purpose.

The movement we needed to become part of in order to allow writing to show its own embedded intelligence, so that we might dance and smear tracks over the paper, would consist of ruptures and breaks, of halting breath and the breathing of silence, of the attempt to recognize pressure points and patterns, of envisioning the future and inventing ourselves—into the past as well; of trying to give the contents an ethical coloring. If the movement were to materialize, it would consist of sedimentation as opposed to stratification.

Maybe the sense of presence was to be darkened. The mirror (the Middle World) was also a screen between the ephemeral *here* always in movement on the page and the beyond of the *not-that*, both re-flection and go-between allowing "internity" and eternity to flow and inform. Maybe the last dance was in the black light of mirror, from where death looked at us with blinding eyes.

For what I'm saying is this: between the inscrutably fortuitous need of birth and the absurd inevitability of death only nothing took on the patterns of meaning. Writing is making nothingness.

ALSO FROM HAYMARKET BOOKS

Between the Lines: Readings on Israel, the Palestinians, and the U.S. "War on Terror"

Tikva Honig-Parnass and Toufic Haddad • This compilation of essays, edited by a Palestinian writer and an Israeli journalist, constitutes a challenge to critically rethink the Israeli-Palestinian conflict. • ISBN 9781931859448

Breaking the Sound Barrier

Amy Goodman, Edited by Denis Moynihan • Amy Goodman, award-winning host of the daily internationally broadcast radio and television program *Democracy Now!*, breaks through the corporate media's lies, sound bites, and silence in this wide-ranging new collection of articles. • ISBN 9781931859998

Class Struggle and Resistance in Africa

Edited By Leo Zeilig • Employing Marxist theory to address the postcolonial problems of several different countries, experts analyze such issues as the renewal of Islamic fundamentalism in Egypt, debt relief, trade union movements, and strike action. Includes interviews with leading African socialists and activists • ISBN 9781931859684

Diary of Bergen Belsen: 1944–1945

Hanna Lévy-Hass, foreword by Amira Hass • Hanna Levy-Hass stands alone as the only resistance fighter to record on her own experience inside the camps, and she does so with unflinching clarity and attention to the political and social divisions inside Bergen Belsen. • ISBN 9781931859875

Essays

Wallace Shawn • In these beautiful essays acclaimed playwright and beloved actor Wallace Shawn takes readers on a revelatory journey through high art, war, politics, culture, and privilege. • ISBN 9781608460021

Exile: Conversations with Pramoedya Ananta Toer

Andre Vltchek, Rosie Indira, edited by Nagesh Rao • This is the first ever book-length interview with Pramoedya, a novelist and writer widely regarded as the artist who gave expression to a revolutionary vision of Indonesian cultural identity. • ISBN 9781931859288

Field Notes on Democracy: Listening to Grasshoppers

Arundhati Roy • Combining fierce conviction, deft political analysis, and beautiful writing, this essential new book from Arundhati Roy examines the dark side of democracy in contemporary India. Roy looks closely at how religious majoritarianism, cultural nationalism, and neo-fascism simmer just under the surface of a country that projects itself as the world's largest democracy. • ISBN 9781608460243

Hopes and Prospects

Noam Chomsky • The Americas, both North and South, have been in motion with elections and political shifts that Noam Chomsky explores here with his characteristic independence and insight. • ISBN 9781931859967

In Praise of Barbarians: Essays Against Empire

Mike Davis • No writer in the United States today brings together analysis and history as comprehensively and elegantly as Mike Davis. The author of *City of Quartz* and *Planet of Slums* attacks the current fashion for empires and white men's burdens in this blistering collection of radical essays. • ISBN 9781931859424

Literature and Revolution

Leon Trotsky, foreword by William Keach • Leon Trotsky penned this engaging book to elucidate the complex way in which art informs—and can alter—our understanding of the world. This new edition features an essay and full explanatory notes from Brown University English professor William Keach. • ISBN 9781931859165

Poetry and Protest: A Dennis Brutus Reader

Dennis Brutus, edited by Aisha Karim and Lee Sustar • This vital original collection of interviews, poetry, and essays of the much-loved anti-apartheid leader is the first book of its kind to bring together the full, forceful range of his work. • ISBN 9781931859226

ABOUT HAYMARKET BOOKS

Haymarket Books is a nonprofit, progressive book distributor and publisher, a project of the Center for Economic Research and Social Change. We believe that activists need to take ideas, history, and politics into the many struggles for social justice today. Learning the lessons of past victories, as well as defeats, can arm a new generation of fighters for a better world. As Karl Marx said, "The philosophers have merely interpreted the world; the point, however, is to change it."

We take inspiration and courage from our namesakes, the Haymarket Martyrs, who gave their lives fighting for a better world. Their 1886 struggle for the eight-hour day, which gave us May Day, the international workers' holiday, reminds workers around the world that ordinary people can organize and struggle for their own liberation. These struggles continue today across the globe—struggles against oppression, exploitation, hunger, and poverty.

It was August Spies, one of the Martyrs targeted for being an immigrant and an anarchist, who predicted the battles being fought to this day. "If you think that by hanging us you can stamp out the labor movement," Spies told the judge, "then hang us. Here you will tread upon a spark, but here, and there, and behind you, and in front of you, and everywhere, the flames will blaze up. It is a subterranean fire. You cannot put it out. The ground is on fire upon which you stand."

We could not succeed in our publishing efforts without the generous financial support of our readers. Many people contribute to our project through the Haymarket Sustainers program, where donors receive free books in return for their monetary support. If you would like to be a part of this program, please contact us at info@haymarketbooks.org. Shop our full catalog and order online at www.haymarketbooks.org.